"NO" Is a Love Word!

"NO"
Is a
Love
Word!

(formerly entitled **Raise Your Kids Right**)

Dr. Lonnie Carton

Learning Center Publications
Newton, Massachusetts

Copyright © 1992 by Dr. Lonnie Carton

Library of Congress Cataloging in Publication Data
Library of Congress Catalog Card Number 91-77338

Carton, Lonnie Caming, date.
"NO" is a Love Word!
(formerly entitled Raise Your Kids Right)

1. Children — Management.   1. Title
HQ769C3415   649'.1   91-77338
ISBN 0-9627183-0-0

Printed in the United States of America

Learning Center Publications
P.O. Box 204
Newtown Branch
Boston, MA 02158

GETTING THE "NO"-HOW

If you know how to say it

FAIRLY
FIRMLY
CALMLY
CONSISTENTLY

"NO" IS A LOVE WORD

For a long time psychologists have known that "THE SET-TING OF LIMITS" satisfies a basic human need: THE NEED FOR STRUCTURE.

All human beings have this need for order and behavioral boundaries. Children and adults alike seek the SECURITY provided by rules and discipline. But despite these "facts of life," many men and women cannot say "NO" at the right time, in the right place, to the right people. They fear that if they do set limits, they will become unpopular or unloved.

Learning how to say "NO" to your child, (to other adults, and even to yourself) is more important today than ever before. WHY? Because we are living in a "YES" society. Instant gratification is everywhere — encouraged or accepted on television, in movies, in magazines and books, as well as in everyday life. The messages that are all too frequently practiced are: "If it feels good, do it!" "Make sure you get yours!" "Get it now!" Unfortunately, the voice of the "yea-sayers" is so loud and persuasive that it drowns out the voice of truth — the truth that "NO" IS A LOVE WORD. Without it, our sons and daughters will grow up WITHOUT SELF CONTROL, WITHOUT SELF-ESTEEM, AND WITHOUT SOCIAL RESPONSIBILITY.

ACKNOWLEDGEMENTS

No one starts anything from his own beginning. All of us are dependent upon the efforts of those whose genesis preceded ours. This book would not have had the authenticity and substance to take shape were it not for the research of psychologists and psychiatrists such as A. H. Maslow, Erik Erikson, Robert Coles, B. F. Skinner, A. S. Neill, Uri Bronfenbrenner and William Glasser to mention only the most prestigious. Their keen clinical understanding of human nature and the social fabric of these days of our lives contributed very significantly to the creation of **"NO" is a Love Word.**

I am also indebted to the many adults and children who provided me opportunities to engage in my own research. My sincere thanks is extended to them for serving as my teachers, friends, guides and followers in the always fruitful, sometimes frustrating process by which I learned about child-rearing and family living firsthand. To Brooks Lane for nurturing the roots, to my supportive husband Ed for nourishing the fledgling flower, to our children Evan, Deborah, Paula, Janis and Joseph for providing the bloom, I am humbly appreciative.

A special kudo to Dr. Evan B. Carton of the English faculty at the University of Texas, Austin, for his perceptive critique of my work in its many stages of development and for his editorial help in making this book say more clearly and concisely what I would like to say.

LONNIE CARTON

To

SHIRLEY COOPER CAMING

my mother,
for loving me, listening to me,
limiting me and letting me go.

CONTENTS

PREFACE

Since 1975, when I became a CBS broadcast journalist heard coast-to-coast by millions of listeners, I have been privileged to share my child-rearing ideas and training with mothers, fathers, grandparents, teachers, and children themselves. My listeners graciously gave me their attention and their trust. In return, I have taken my responsibility as a "friend of the family" very seriously. I have tried to provide simply stated, "usable" information and insights to help adults and children better understand, support, and enjoy each other.

This book combines three of the skills which have made THE LEARNING CENTER broadcasts so successful. The first is the result of my many years of professional education and research in the area of human growth and development. The second is my "on-the-job" training as a wife, mother and grandmother. The third quality is a combination of two senses which we all learn in one way or another are essential to any human relationship, particularly the adult-child relationship: COMMON SENSE and a SENSE OF HUMOR.

My own sense of humor was tested when on many occasions our own children would come home and report that they had been asked questions such as: "Tell me the truth now, is Dr. Lonnie Carton really a good mother, herself?" With combined pride and humility, I believe their answers supported the fact that what is written within the pages of this book is a reliable, workable guide to rearing self-disciplined, self-reliant, secure, socially responsible human beings.

Reading my manuscript, the oldest of our children remarked: "It is a great book, Mom, but I'm not sure there's anything new in it. It is exactly the way you treated us when we were young." For the most part, it is...except for all the things the children themselves taught me. Looking back, I have a much richer understanding of why our eight-year old once decided to run away from home; what each child experienced at the death of a beloved grandmother and grandfather; and how all their successes and failures in relationships with friends and teachers have affected their lives.

"No" is a Love Word! is an effort to describe how the balance between what children need and what adults need can be found; how each can live fuller, happier lives, together and separately.

The "SEVEN 'NO'S' STRATEGY" developed in these pages conveys all the important things known about human growth and development. Beginning with the certainty that total freedom for either adult or child is total chaos, it is possible to discard both *hit therapy* and *halo therapy*. Neither has worked well in the past, nor will either work in today's complex world. *Heart-head therapy* does work! It combines the normal feelings of affection in our hearts with the common sense in our heads. The information and insights gained make it possible to give boys and girls the fair, firm, consistent, caring discipline they need and want.

COMMENTS AND VIEWS ON DR. LONNIE CARTON

Some Of The Honors and Awards Bestowed Upon
Dr. Lonnie Carton

1985 **The Maggie Award** – ''for excellence in media coverage of reproductive health and rights issues''
– Seattle; Margaret Sanger Society

1988 **Don Bosco Centennial Award** – ''for outstanding dedication to youth''
– Salesian Society of America

1988 **Massachusetts Society for the Prevention of Cruelty to Children** – ''for services rendered for children and families in Massachusetts''

...at an In-service Program for **teachers,** followed by an evening program for **parents** sponsored by the **Governor's Alliance Against Drugs Advisory Council-**...''Teachers enjoyed your comments about the emotional health of youngsters...and building (their) self-esteem. Parents were treated to practical advice on how to get along with their teenagers.''
– Superintendent of Public Schools

''Dr. Carton communicates with directness, understanding and humor...''
– Parent Education Resources Collaborative

1.

BEGINNING WITH COMMON SENSE

"Who are you?" said the Caterpillar.
. . . Alice replied, rather shyly, "I—I hardly know,
sir, just at present—at least, I know who I was when I
got up this morning, but I think I must have changed
several times since then."

When Lewis Carroll wrote this dialogue in *Alice's Adventures in Wonderland*, he could not have known that he was describing the feeling of many twentieth-century parents. "I know who I was when I got up this morning, but I . . . must have been changed several times since then."

Just as Alice was bewildered when she found herself in a strange land, many men and women are perplexed by parenthood. Day by day, they are changed by the energy-draining, dollar-consuming, time-demanding responsibilities of raising children. Little wonder that many parents feel confused, frustrated, angry. Their inability to become the competent, contented parents they would like to be embarrasses and annoys them.

Most annoying of all is the bewilderment mothers and fathers feel about disciplining children. Do boys and girls of all ages require control? When limits are set, should these be firm and unchangeable, or open to question by those required to obey them? Is the same kind of disciplinary action right for all children? Will the imposition of behavioral restrictions destroy a child's creativity? Will it make him fearful or angry?

A disciplinary dilemma for many adults is, "Will saying 'no' to my youngster cause him to love me less?"

No one has yet found a "fits-all-sizes" solution to the question of discipline. The amount of attention, affection, and affirmation a child needs, or a parent can give, varies with each individual. There are, however, certain psychologically sound attitudes and commonsense skills which any parent can learn easily. Using these guidelines will make living with children of any age more successful and more satisfying.

The purpose of this book is to help YOU transform the job of parenthood into a joy. No matter how you are functioning now, this is not an impossible dream! Adults and children alike are remarkably resilient. Both are not only capable of change, but willing and anxious to try a new or a different road if it promises to lead to greater security and fulfillment.

The road to a happy, healthy parent-child relationship is made much smoother if adults know when and how to discipline their children. Developing this insight requires that they take a close look at some of the day-to-day problems and pressures involved in child rearing.

BASIC TRAINING

I am desperate to get my three-year-old son out of diapers. My neighbors keep asking me why he's so slow. They know my other child was only two when trained, and their kids took care of themselves long before they reached three. People make me feel like it's my fault that he's not trained, but I don't know what I'm doing wrong. The worst part is that when my husband sees our boy mess himself, he shouts at him, "You're too big for that nonsense." Usually, he whips the child, too. What should I do?

If any whipping is warranted, it's the father, not the son who deserves it! Messy and irritating as an untrained child may be, when a youngster's social behavior is linked with a biological function over which he may have no conscious control, adults should look before they leap on him. Physically or psychologically beating a child down with the pressure of adult anger is cruel and unnatural punishment. It says NO firmly, but not fairly.

No child, especially a preschooler, should be compared with an older child, a neighbor's child, or anyone else. He is himself, and that is who he should be allowed to be. If his better-trained sibling or the child of the busybody neighbor is female, then comparisons are particularly odious; it's fair to say that girls usually develop faster than boys, physically, socially, and emotionally. Girls are notorious for being out of diapers more quickly than their male counterparts.

The best way to say "no" to a child in basic training is to regularly take him to the bathroom several times a day. He should be encouraged to sit there for a reasonable length of time, five or ten minutes, while calmly being given a clear understanding of what he is expected to accomplish. Neither the tone of the adult's voice nor the timing should make the child feel rushed or frightened. And, not Mommy or Daddy, or anyone else, should allow the boy to jump up and down or avoid giving his best effort to the job at hand. If the child is permitted to look at books or listen to records while "waiting," he must be made to understand that looking and listening are not the main things upon which he should be concentrating his attention. Whenever the child is successful, he should be praised.

Because preschoolers try to please parents and do what they are told is "right," patience and friendly persuasion work better than punishment. No matter what kind of training parents instill in their offspring, its success should be measured on two counts—the child's accomplishment and the price paid. Training a child to fear, mistrust, or dislike the adult applying discipline is too high a price to pay for any accomplishment!

WINNING THUMBS-DOWN?

Our six-year-old has a habit that I can't stand. She chews on, licks, loudly sucks, and practically "cannibalizes" her thumb. It is particularly disgusting when we are at a friend's home or have people over to our house. We have whipped her, put bad tasting medicine on her fingers, ridiculed her for such babyish behavior, but we still don't seem able to stop her.

Before deciding what to do about a child's behavior, parents should find out *why* the child is engaging in it. A child of six, who has been continually sucking her thumb since she was two or three, may merely be continuing what comes naturally. Her early habit, uncorrected and uncontrolled, became a necessity.

In the preschool years, a youngster may take comfort in his thumb as the friend always at hand, the one on whom he can depend. On the other hand, a child may thumb-suck to satisfy a purely physical need. The normal sucking urge with which babies are born does not exhaust itself in some children until they are three or more. The less sucking satisfaction the baby received at bottle or breast, the more need that child may have as a toddler, when the drinking cup replaces the nipple.

By the time a child is of school age, thumb-sucking is less likely to be related to physical need. More often, it is the security blanket of psychological need. Children who feel lonely, afraid, or neglected often seek their thumb for solace. Before turning thumbs-down on the thumb-sucking child, adults should try to understand and alleviate the CAUSE of the irritating habit as well as the SYMPTOM.

Sometimes a child sucks his thumb, bites other children, or uses foul language merely to attract adult attention. It is a way of saying, "Look at me, stop ignoring me."

If this is the goal of the child who "chews on, licks, . . . and practically 'cannibalizes' her thumb," hers is a real success story. She has succeeded in getting people to pay attention to her even though she had to be whipped and ridiculed to do it.

Children who feel ignored will go to any length to be recognized. The urge to belong and to be acknowledged is a basic human need. Hitting, shouting at, or embarrassing children gives them, in a negative manner, exactly what they're asking for—attention.

Counteracting this "attention-at-any-cost" action by children is not difficult. Mothers and fathers need only tell it like it is, clearly and calmly: The child must learn that no longer will anybody in the family watch a display of inappropriate behavior now that the child has been warned to cease and desist. Should the youngster persist in the undesirable action, that child will find himself performing for the four walls of his own room.

Whenever parents reprimand a child, they should also inform him of the acceptable ways to get what he wants. If attention is desired, if the child feels lonely and neglected, the youngster should be encouraged to signal this in nonoffensive ways. The girl in our example might learn to move physically closer to mother or father, reach out to hold a hand, or wait for a break in the adult conversation or preoccupation to ask for a few moments "all her own." If she knows how to write, she might be asked to slip a written message to the parents reminding them of her desire to be both seen and heard.

Giving children alternatives and praising them, rather than blaming them, whenever possible, is more likely to elicit acceptable behavior. In any conflict or compromise with youngsters, what is important is not so much what an adult says or does, but whether what is said or done is communicated in an atmosphere of light rather than in heat.

THIS PROPERTY IS CONDEMNED

Whenever my seven-year-old brings a playmate home, everything in the house except the kitchen sink gets dragged out. I have no complaints about their playing with everything but I do get upset when the visitor leaves. My daughter takes one long look at all the cleaning up that has to be done, and she begins to fret. She claims she's tired or she very, very slowly puts a few things away. Before I know it, it's dinner time or her bedtime, and I'm left holding the bag, the trash bag. I've yelled at her enough about this, but I still can't seem to avoid being left with a house that looks like a cyclone struck it.

If a word (or two) to the wise is sufficient, parents need to "Get Smart!" No child should be permitted to take advantage of anyone, particularly a parent. Parents are people, too, a fact of which children large and small need to be reminded. Just as youngsters have needs and wants, likes and dislikes, so do mothers and fathers. The preferences and priorities of parents must be respected, too.

To gain respect from children, adults should give respect—not only to the youngsters, but to themselves. Parents who think so little of their own worth that they allow themselves to serve as doormats for children have no one but themselves to blame when they are walked all over.

No child of any age should be allowed to walk away from responsibilities, unless the child is too ill to fulfill them. Being sick and tired of doing an unpleasant or boring job—like cleaning up—doesn't count as a valid excuse. Whether a child is made to stay up past bedtime, miss an important party, or lose an allowance, he should still be required to do what is expected of him, and what he should ultimately come to expect of himself.

Nowhere in life are there rights without responsibilities. It is never too early to teach a child fairly, firmly, consistently, and without guilt, that only those willing to give will be given the right to take.

What the parent of the seven-year-old housewrecker should give the daughter each time she takes out "everything except the kitchen sink" is a little alarm clock. Setting it to a time corresponding to ten or fifteen minutes before her playmate is scheduled to leave (or, if she is playing alone, before her bed, bath, or mealtime), Mother should forewarn the child that the alarm is the signal for putting things away. No matter how much "stuff" needs putting back in place or how tired the little housekeepers get, she must do her job. Since misery loves company, the clean-up may even be done quickly if her playmate is included.

Forewarning children is the best way to forearm them. Should the playmate beat the clock by having to go home early, the little hostess with the mostest should clearly understand that she, not her mother, will be left "holding the bag—the trash bag."

UNEMPLOYMENT

The thing that bugs me most about our twelve-year-old is that he's lazy. He can see dishes in the sink piled almost to the ceiling, wade through grass or snow up to his boot tops, or watch a pot boil over. He can hear a telephone ring, or see a newspaper getting rained on, and he will never lift himself up to give a helping hand. I've tried yelling, hitting, punishing. So what do I do now?

Not enough parents calmly and carefully tell a child his help is NEEDED! It is not only desired and requested; it is needed. Explaining to the "lazy" teenager that the amount of work that must be done for a family to function requires that everyone pitch in to do a fair share is the best way to get him to do his.

Too often, children of all ages are allowed to float through their homes on a cloud of oblivion. From this position, they are unable to see what needs doing. Hard working mothers and fathers often make life look so easy that the child assumes things fall into place and work automatically. For all he knows, meals are cooked, clothes washed and ironed, broken things repaired, and money supplied by a friendly genie emerging from a magic lamp. No one takes the time to sit down with the child and explain how the real world operates. No one impresses upon him that *his* effort is needed in order for the family to function.

Disciplining children wisely and well requires that they be brought down to earth. This does not mean robbing them of their childhood or callously pulling them up by the bootstraps. Children need to be needed; they need to feel they amount to something as participating members of a group effort. Whether that group is the family or the baseball team, those who feel a sense of belonging rarely strike out.

Because "life is real and life is earnest," it is never too late in the life of a child to tell it like it is. When time and thought and affection are put into the telling, children don't have to be told over and over again what is expected of them; they rarely need to be reminded how much their effort is needed. Just as

22

all work and no play makes Jack a dull boy, allowing all play and no work places his maturation in jeopardy. He is denied the experience necessary to develop into a competent, self-reliant, cooperative individual.

THE DATING GAME

Do you think a father should have a say over the boys who take out his daughter? She is fifteen, mature for her age, physically and socially. She goes out on movie dates and also attends mixed parties at friends' homes. Whenever I ask her who she's going out with or whether I can meet the boy she plans to get together with at the donut shop or at the party, she gets angry. She accuses me of being nosy and old-fashioned, insisting that no other fathers demand all this information. She claims I don't trust her. I still feel I have a right to know who she is out with.

Parents have a right to know, with no two ways about it. To give a teenager unrestricted freedom often gets everybody nowhere.

A father's or mother's interest in a youngster's whereabouts is natural and necessary, not nosy or old-fashioned. Whether the child is five or fifteen, she should be expected to show the same trust in her parents as she wants them to have in her. Unless adults have repeatedly proven themselves unworthy of this trust, a child should be expected to bring friends home. Only if she's ashamed of her friends or ashamed of her family is there reason for her to insist that never the twain shall meet.

Most adolescents are in a stage of their life when they are betwixt and between. They are caught in the middle of their

23

desire for independence and their need for dependence. During these teenage years, a second umbilical cord is being cut; parent and child are undergoing normal and necessary emotional and social separation. This developmental process heightens the adolescent's demand for privilege and privacy.

While the demand for privacy should be conscientiously respected by adults, it needs to be done with the full understanding by the child that such privacy is not the same as secrecy. A calm exchange of ideas between parent and adolescent is the best way to bring the difference out in the open. The child should be given an opportunity to explain, in detail, why it is so important to him to refuse to divulge the information sought. The teenager must be reminded of the many areas of privacy he does enjoy. No one opens his mail, searches through his bedroom drawers or spies on his telephone conversations. Nor is a teenager expected to take a chaperone along when he goes out to parties or mixes with his peers. In exchange for these rights, the adolescent has the responsibility to voluntarily share with his parents the information they require—about the friends he keeps and the activities in which he engages—providing this information does not curtail his privacy nor limit him. What it does is supply interested, caring parents with some of the inside information they have a right to know. No matter how big teenagers are, or think they are, these boys and girls are still their parents' children. They need and deserve parental guidance, support, and structure. No chip off the old block should be left totally on his own to let the rest of the chips fall where they may. Unguided children are too susceptible to getting into difficulty and danger.

Not only common sense, but common courtesy, requires that parents know what their children are doing, and with whom. It's a sign of a child's maturity that he or she understand and accept this fact of life. Lacking such maturity, the youngster is probably not yet old enough to be allowed the right to as much privacy as he demands.

MAN-CHILD IN THE PROMISED LAND

When our son, a sophomore in college, comes home on vacation, he frequently brings a friend with him. Some of the friends are male, some female. On the last trip he invited a girl he has been dating a month or so at school. Quite naturally, when it came time to assign sleeping space, I showed her to the guest room on the first floor. When my son got me alone he said, "Look, Mom, who's kidding whom? Suzanne and I are sleeping together at college so what's this about putting her in the guest room? Both of us are going to sleep in my room." I was shocked. I opened my mouth to say something, but nothing came out. Is a parent just expected to grin and bear it when an older child insists on doing something with which the parent doesn't agree?

Adults should not be forced to grin and bear a child's unbearable behavior. Nor should they be obliged to give in or give way to his manner of doing things. Only when parents voluntarily come around to their youngster's way of thinking should they follow his lead.

Mothers and fathers who permit children to lead them around by the nose invariably get taken for a ride—a guilt trip. By innuendo or outspoken criticism, young people make the older generation feel like has-beens. The pressure to accept the new morality or the new methodology of behavior and to "get with it" really gets to parents. They fear losing their child's respect or love if they do not capitulate to his every whim or wish.

To be a good parent requires many sacrifices, among them the sacrificing of time, energy, money. One sacrifice parents should never make is that of their own values. Whatever mothers and fathers value—social attitudes, economic concepts, political beliefs—they have a right to stand up for what they feel is right.

Should college or high school students find it comfortable to sleep together in college dorms, or elsewhere, that may be their privilege. It is parental privilege, however, to set the standards with which mothers and fathers feel comfortable in their own homes. Adults should make this point of privilege clear to young people in a nonjudgmental, inoffensive way. This is the best way to handle the differences in living style between generations.

Whether the friendly persuasion applied is that "A man's home is his castle" or "When in Rome, do as the Romans do," the young need to be made to realize that they cannot have everything their own way. From preschooler to adult, humans must learn to compromise, to give a little and take a little, to develop the ability to forego instant gratification, when necessary. To help them, it is frequently necessary for parents to stand up to their children. By standing for something rather than bending over backwards to satisfy every whine or whim of a child, parents provide him with the support he needs to grow toward self-discipline.

Among the many skills and attitudes parents need to develop in their effort to know when and how to discipline their children, these are some of the important ones exemplified by the case studies in this chapter.

1. Look before you leap on children. Find out what physical, social, emotional, or other needs motivate them before deciding what action to take.

2. Don't substitute "carbon copy solutions" for the real thing. No child is identical to others of his age or group. Comparisons are dangerous, unless they ac-

knowledge the normality of differences as well as similarities in youngsters.

3. Use praise more than blame whenever possible. Praising children encourages them to work with you. Blaming them conditions them to work against you.

4. Guide in light rather than in heat. Tone and volume of voice as well as the particular words chosen can either cool off conflict between parent and child or add more fuel to the fire.

5. Avoid head-on collisions. Recognize that a good parent-child relationship is a two-way street. When a child's behavior is unacceptable, try to show him an alternative route to take in getting what he wants or needs.

6. Recognize that parents are people, too. Adults who allow themselves to become doormats for children get walked all over. The needs and rights of parents for attention, affection, and affirmation must be respected.

7. Tell it like it is. The efforts of everyone in a family are needed in order for it to function. All in the family, including children, have responsibilities as well as rights. Youngsters should be expected to do their fair share.

2.

WHAT DO I DO NOW?

Children's literature contains many examples of young people who did, or tried to do, their fair share. One of the most famous of these is the little Dutch boy who saved his village from being flooded by putting his finger into the hole in the dike. This youngster's efforts were credited with keeping the water from flooding the town until help could be summoned to repair the leak.

Perhaps the incident portrayed in the story never really happened. If it did, there must have been a moment of truth in which the little Dutch boy saw the hole in the dike, realized the danger, and asked himself, "What do I do now?"

Although the circumstances are different, it is this question which many parents ask themselves whenever they confront the real or potential danger of undisciplined children. What do I do now to discipline Joan for back talking, for hitting her sister, for lying? What do I do now, before it's too late, to keep Andy out of the street, in school, or off alcohol, tobacco, and drugs? What do I do now to help my children learn from their mistakes, not merely learn not to get caught? What do I do now to show Joan and Andy that it's not THEY who are bad or dumb, it's their BEHAVIOR?

Everyone who has ever tried to understand, live with, or teach children has asked this question. The way they have answered it has depended upon two things—the method of discipline they had been using up to that time, and the reasons they had been using it.

Before all mothers, fathers, grandparents, teachers and other adults interested in children can successfully answer the question, "What do I do now?," they need to stop, look, and listen. Relax! Decelerate. People who drive themselves forward too fast often wind up going off in the wrong direction. A look in the rearview mirror to see where you have been coming from can frequently avoid needless wear and tear.

No matter what the direction from which you've been coming, or how far gone you think you are, take a look back. *How have you been disciplining youngsters up to this time?* What do you rely upon to guide you—the advice of professional child developmentalists, tips from your neighbors and relatives, trial and error, or your own common sense? Which strategies for dealing with youngsters work well and which don't—hitting, yelling, embarrassing, ignoring, sermonizing, bribing, reasoning, privilege-denying, praising, or blaming? Have you found that some methods work sometimes but not at other times? Do you ever wonder why the things that worked well with your older child are not working now with a younger one? Do you know whether or not there is any rhyme or reason for the way you discipline?

In the methods of parenting they adopt, adults often do unto others as was done unto them. Many parents who hit children more than they hug them, ridicule them more than they respect them, lecture more than they listen, are only doing what comes naturally. They, themselves, may be the offspring of parents who were constantly punitive. In monkey see, monkey do fashion, parents follow the leader, running around in circles in the same behavioral cycle in which they took part as children. In the rearing of their own offspring, men and women naturally, and often unwittingly, imitate the lessons they learned from their own mothers and fathers. The psychological term for this persuasive and pervasive process of carbon copying is "role modeling."

Role modeling transmits attitudes and actions from one generation to the next. Mothers and fathers tend to carefully follow the direction of those who produced them in the same way actresses and actors follow a script. The adult who looks closely at his or her own actions can often see that he's a chip off the old block, or that like mother, like daughter.

Family habit and happenstance are not the only reasons that you may be doing what you are doing with your children. The great society outside the family, particularly as it is projected by the media, is another powerful, often perilous role modeler. People who shape children's lives are continually bombarded, besieged, and often buffaloed by helpful hints or miracle methods from so-called experts. While most of us need all the help we can get in order to succeed in so difficult a task as rearing children, the help of such experts is often no help at all. Their advice may sound good in theory, but it fails the test on real people. The trouble is that neither these dispensers of the cure-all, nor the people searching for the remedies, take into consideration one basic fact of child rearing— that all children are not alike. Nor are adults. Because of these individual differences, no push-button prescription works. Quite the contrary! Authoritarian disciplining may cause one child to become self-disciplined and productive; it may prompt another to hostile, lazy, hedonistic behavior. Despite this psychological truth, too many advice givers relay their message by prescribing a mass cure for the masses; they treat unique and individual people as if they were carbon copies of one another.

"Love your child" is prescribed indiscriminately both to those parents who are already killing their kids with kindness, as well as to those who can't find anything in the child to love. "Don't let your baby cry it out! Crying may be a sign he's bored. Letting him remain bored could retard his mental growth and creativity," the advice givers warn. The same "group think" is disseminated to the working mother lacking the time or physical energy to run to Johnny every time he cries, as well as to the grandmother or older sister who is spoiling the baby by carrying him around all day to KEEP HIM from crying.

One medication won't cure all illnesses, nor will the same medicine help to relieve a similar illness in different people. The individual physical and emotional differences in humans prescribe what will work best for each. When doctors or other helping hands operate on the basis of a general symptom rather than the specific cause of the illness, they may perform a clinically good operation but the patient, nevertheless, may not recover. Human beings can not be viewed as assembly-line robots, meant to be programmed, controlled, or dehumanized by the button-pushing of others. Nor can they be thought of as empty buckets into which an equal measure and potency of "stuff" recommended for cure can be stuffed.

Each and every person alive is a unique and worthwhile individual and should be treated as such. As humans, we are all members of a species with comparable physical characteristics and social attributes, but, although we share similar emotional needs, we are dissimilar, unique, separate personalities. What works in child rearing for your sister-in-law, your neighbor, or the author of the latest book on "making parenthood paradise," may foul up the works for you. Your problems, your pleasures, your personality, your procedures are distinct from theirs. Where you are functioning in the child-adult relationship—what you are doing now with and to your child and why you are doing it—is an important difference.

Not only are you as a parent different from others, but you become a different parent to each of your children. Mother is a different parent to four-year-old Jimmy than she was to

Bobby when he was that age. Her energy, her experience, and her economic situation may be among the many changed conditions which affect her actions and attitudes. The behavior of father, grandpa, the teacher, or any other adult guiding those who are growing up is similarly the product of feelings, beliefs, habits, and lessons shaped by whatever pressures or pleasures time provides.

Like adults, children—even sisters or brothers who are identical twins—differ markedly. They differ in their predispositions and personalities. They differ in their actions, reactions, and interactions with those around them. Twelve-year-old Claire may act like an angel around father, but she gives mom a devil of a time. Nine-year-old Debbie may feel nobody loves her and threaten to run away. Actually, she gets twice as much attention and affection from the family as her brother Bruce. But he feels very secure in the love and time tendered to him because of his own individual nature.

Human differences within, toward, and between children and adults cause constant change and activity. This flux or instability is not necessarily a disagreeable or destructive situation. Those who know how to handle and balance it can use change constructively; they find living with children exciting and satisfying. Developing the skill to transform the job of parenting into the joy of parenting is no easy task. Nor is it an impossible dream! Those who find motherhood and fatherhood an experience bordering on nightmare can be awakened to a new human interaction, one that results in more "treat" than "trick." They can enjoy a parent-child relationship built upon greater concern, greater communication, greater cooperation among all family members.

To be successful, any human interaction requires that all participants understand and support one another. This relationship, however, cannot be fixed or sterile. Little in human action or reaction remains exactly the same for more than a brief period of time. The solidity and success of parent-child relations depends upon each individual's ability to keep adjusting to change.

The adjusted person is not the individual who has learned some strategies and solutions and lives happily ever after following his system. Adjusted people are those who have acquired the skills and the knowledge to be able to adapt continuously, to grow constantly, and to know what to do or what not to do—whenever the question arises, "What do I do now?"

When chemists and pharmacists mix one substance with another in constant quantities, ten different times, they get the same result or reaction in each case. The mixing and interrelating of human "substances" is never so reliable. Each human being is an individual, and individuals are different from each other and different from other members of their own age group. There is no mold from which all mothers, fathers, teachers, or other adults are cloned, nor is there one model child from which all others are carbon copied. To expand somewhat on William Shakespeare's lines, "All the world's a stage, and all the men and women merely players! They have their exits and their entrances; and one man (and woman and child) in his time plays many parts."

By putting the parts together, carefully and completely, a workable, meaningful, individualized whole can emerge to serve as a basis for a productive parent-child relationship. Because you are unique, and your child is also special, YOU are needed as an active participant in this learning process. It is the process of deciding "What do I do now" each time that question needs asking. It is the procedure for developing a child-rearing structure which may not meet your neighbor's needs or your cousin's expectations, but which will be understandable and satisfying to you and your child.

Getting started in this learning process requires finding out where you are now. But don't worry! Neither a couch nor a series of fifty-minute hours is necessary. Your reaction to only one word will enable you to answer that question.

Before showing you this ten-letter word, a brief explanation! (Please do not leap ahead and see the word in advance before you know what to do with it. Should you do so, you will deny yourself the opportunity to learn where you are coming from in dealing with children, and why.) In the field of psychology, numerous kinds of tests are used. They help the clinician establish some base lines about the client's past experiences, present activities, and future aspirations. There are performance tests, achievement tests, aptitude tests, I.Q. tests, and character and personality tests, to mention but a few. The results of these tests, if reliable and valid, give psychologists important clues about what makes people tick—what they are like, attitude and action wise. Sometimes tests pinpoint specific factors which point to why people do what they do.

Before beginning, put your mind at ease. There are no right or wrong answers. The same ten-letter word test to which you will soon react has been given to hundreds of college students, parents, teachers, and other interested citizens. Countless people of every race, religion, region, and socioeconomic group know the word intimately. So don't worry. No matter what you associate with it, you're bound to have company. The important thing about this experience is to follow the directions carefully. Try hard to associate freely, to relate honestly to the first word, phrase, or idea which comes to your mind the minute your eyes see the key word.

If you'd like a practice round, here is a pretest. Not only will it warm you up for the real thing, but you'll get a better idea of how children feel in school. It's not bad enough that the teacher makes them write twenty spelling words on their list or compute fifteen arithmetic answers every Friday; she makes them do it twice, counting the warm-up or pretest she gives the Monday before!

The next word you see in capital letters will be your pretest word. When you see it, jot down or mentally grab hold of the first idea or word that comes to your mind in response to it. This will be the concept or thing you free associate with the key word. Ready?

The word is BLUE

Over the years, among the free-association responses given to the warm-up word, BLUE, were *boy, sad, Monday, red, bird, funk, nose, blood, a kiss, volcano,* and *wind.* The reason for responses such as *nose, a kiss, volcano,* and *wind* was that the key word was often given orally rather than visually. Some participants heard BLUE as BLEW! In addition to the word responses listed here, there were hundreds of others whose particular connections were meaningful only to the individuals verbally or visually associating with BLUE or BLEW.

Now for the real thing—the ten-letter word which should enable each reader to discover his or her own starting point to answer the question, "What do I do now?" Again you will see, when you turn the page, a word in capital letters. Look at it carefully. Then write down immediately or mentally hold onto the associated word or idea that the key word prompts. To do this as scientifically as possible under the circumstances, try to clear your mind of all other thoughts. To help do this, before you turn the page, close your eyes and clear your head.

DISCIPLINE

If your free association with the word DISCIPLINE caused you to think or write words like *control, restrict, hate, punish, hit, shout,* or similar words considered to be harsh, unpleasant, or punitive, welcome to the club. Your response agrees with the majority opinion. Even if your matching word was *teacher, school, principal, mother, father,* or *grandparent,* and you regard these people as punishers, you get to join the crowd. Well over 70 percent of all the people responding to this free-association stimulus think of the word "discipline" in negative terms. (Later in this chapter, an explanation will be given as to why the "Hit 'Em Again Harder" connection scored the most points.)

If you reacted to the ten-letter key word with words like *love, help,* or *security,* you are in the silent minority. Even if you responded with words like *teacher, mother,* or *father,* and associated these people with kind, helping hands rather than with "hitting hands," you join the 20 percent who view discipline positively. The missing percentage of participants taking the test gave answers which could not be easily categorized as either positive or negative. Words such as *philosophy* (from a college student majoring in that field or discipline), or *work, people,* and *life* represented various personal connections. Understanding the meaning behind your choice should provide an individual starting point for you. It can help you learn something about why you are doing what you are doing to your children, for your children, and with your children.

Some adults who associate the word DISCIPLINE with hitting, haranguing, or ridiculing automatically gravitate to that method of dealing with young people. What they are doing is what comes naturally. By physically and verbally implementing their concept of keeping children in line, they respond punitively to all types of misbehavior. Conditioned by whatever forces make adults what *they* are, these parents and teachers possess a method mind-set. Whether or not the method fits their child, or any child, does not matter. They misuse their energy and their children trying to fit the person to the method rather than the method to the person. Even some parents who admit they would not be successful in pushing a square peg into a round hole continue pushing their children around. Some do it in an effort to get even with the child for daring to defy adult authority. The child has misbehaved; he must be disciplined for it, and discipline is synonymous with stern, strict physical and psychological retribution.

Unlike these parents, there are many who talk tough or think tough, but who don't follow through. Not everybody practices what he preaches. Merely because you, yourself, related discipline to dictatorship does not necessarily mean that you "practice" slapping, shouting, harassing, or harshly controlling children. Quite the opposite may be true. Many adults who regard discipline as punitive, negative, or authoritarian never lay a hand on a child. Still able to feel the sting of oppression or embarrassment they suffered at the hands of the adults who reared them, these mothers and fathers make a determined effort *not* to follow in their own parents' footsteps. They carefully control their inclination to lay it on the child when he misbehaves. They exert a tremendous effort to be better, more benevolent caretakers of the young than were their own mothers and fathers.

Some of these caring, good-natured grown-ups who refrain from any kind of disciplining at all can still hurt children seriously. They kill them with kindness—the kindness of permissiveness. In their effort to get youngsters out from under the thumb of repressive discipline, these parents permit children to thumb their noses at all adult direction and restraint. Such guardians unwittingly deny children one of their most fundamental needs—the need for STRUCTURE.

In the name of loving children, some adults love them and leave them. They leave young people totally on their own to

37

find their own direction and to attain and maintain their own discipline. Often, parents grin and bear youngsters' unacceptable actions and words rather than bear down on them. Because these grown-ups have not grown wise enough to realize the importance of extending the helping hand of guidance to the young, they throw up their hands in helplessness. They can't say "no," even though that is the only way to guide children toward developing more self-disciplined and socially responsible behavior.

Guiding, setting limits, and developing structure for children is one of the major tasks for which mature adults are responsible. Parents and teachers who transfer this obligation to the immature, inexperienced young may love children well, but not wisely.

To love youngsters wisely and well, adults must discipline them. Discipline, regardless of what word it brought to your mind, actually means GUIDANCE. Discipline is neither a no-no word nor a word connoting oppression. Discipline is a fact of life for all people, especially children. It is a love word: the fair, firm, consistent guidance adults who love and respect children take the time to give them. Disciplining young people of all ages is both the right and the responsibility of parents and teachers who care for and about children. To do the job *right* requires knowing not only what kind of discipline to use, but how much, and when.

Establishing a parent-child relationship that is fulfilling for adults as well as satisfying to the younger generation requires finding a happy balance between totalitarian control of children's lives and total surrender to their will or whim.

Since actions speak at least as loudly as words, your particular association earlier in this chapter is hardly our only concern. Whether you associated DISCIPLINE with hugging or hitting, embarrassing or embracing, bribing or belting, the crucial issue now is what you are actually doing in child rearing, and why. These are some of the questions you need to ask in order to discover for yourself, WHAT DO I DO NOW?

38

1. Are your methods and disciplinary philosophy a carbon copy of the ones used on you?

2. Do you recall your own childhood mostly with pleasure, or with pain?

3. Is your present relationship with your youngsters the kind you would "want to write home about"?

4. Has the world changed enough in the generation between you and your youngster that you need to find additional or alternative skills and strategies for disciplining?

Anyone who deals with children has three general choices in giving them guidance. He or she may use hit therapy, halo therapy, or heart-head therapy. In the following chapters, these methods will be discussed. It will be shown how living with children can be satisfying and successful when adults know what to expect from children, and children know what to expect in return.

3.

HIT AND MISS DESPERATION

There was an old woman who lived in a shoe; she had so many children, she didn't know what to do.

Not only in nursery rhymes, but in real life, the responsibility of having to care for many children, or even just one, can prove confusing and frustrating. By their nature, children demand a tremendous amount of adult time and effort. They need attention, affection, affirmation, and discipline. Often, parents find themselves in short supply of the patience and skill needed to satisfy children's demands. For many adults, the world is too much with them. They feel caught in the middle, torn between responsibility to their offspring and the right to live their "own" lives more fully, indulging their own adult interests and needs. Invariably, the personal desires of grown-ups—for mature friendships, leisure and recreational activities, and even their own careers—compete for the limited time and energy available in a day or a week. More often

41

than not, being Eddie's mother or Debbie's dad must, of necessity, win the tug of war, even though that may not be the direction in which the adult prefers to be pulled.

Managing to meet a child's physical needs for food, clothing, and shelter usually can be accomplished, even by busy parents; providing adequate psychological nourishment is much more difficult. When children misbehave, harried parents tend to resort to the same desperate child-rearing practices as the old woman who lived in the shoe. What she wound up doing with her annoyingly dependent brood was to give them some milk and give them some bread, then whip them all soundly and put them to bed.

Whether whipping children soundly is the most suitable way to rear them is a dilemma which parents have debated for a long time. Does it teach children not to misbehave, or merely not to get caught? Are children punished as painfully by words as by wallops? How does hitting affect the child's self-image and the way he interacts with his siblings, friends, and relatives.

Hit therapy is one of the oldest methods of disciplining the young. In our country, its roots go back to the child-rearing practices of Colonial times. The religious beliefs of the Puritans prescribed that to spare the rod was to spoil the child. Adults were mandated to save children from going to hell in the hereafter by knocking the hell out of them on earth. Youngsters who did not obey the schoolmaster promptly and perfectly were beaten with a birch switch, or whatever else he could lay his hands on. Pupils who talked too much had whispering sticks stuck in their mouths. These not only stopped the child from talking, but they made him look like a horse with a bit between his teeth. The sight caused the erring child to be subjected to insufferable ridicule from his classmates. Some bad children even had yokes put over their heads and were forced to stand in front of the class like harnessed animals. Whenever pupils failed to do their lessons well, they were made to sit on a high stool and wear a cone-shaped cap with the word DUNCE printed on it. In the home, disobedience was also met with whipping, denial of food and warm shelter, ridicule, isolation, and other harsh punishments.

The popular appeal of spanking, whipping, shouting, and ridiculing has not significantly diminished over the last two centuries. Not only out in the field but also at home base, the cry to hit 'em again harder is not unfamiliar. Believing that the best defense is a strong offense, many parents hit children from every direction, verbally and physically. Some hit hard, some less forcefully. The physical punishment they inflict ranges from an occasional swat across the seat to frequent heavy-handed, rear-reddening spankings, and even assaults on other parts of the body.

Not only are disobedient children assailed with wallops, they are stung with words used in loud, abusive criticism, ridicule, and sarcasm. These onslaughts cause children emotional hurt, just as hands or straps inflict physical pain. On the surface, physical punishment is quick, easy, and successful. With one blow, mothers and fathers not only let off their own steam, they douse the unacceptable behavioral outburst of the youngster. A slap or wallop rarely misses its mark. Swiftly and surely, it gets to the offending child's back, face, hands, or seat. Unfortunately, neither hitting nor verbally assailing the child gets to the root of the problem.

The problem with many misbehaving children is that they suffer from growing pains. Merely by doing what comes naturally, the youngster becomes a pain in the neck to adults. Without understanding the child's motivation, grown-ups frequently respond defensively. They fight fire with fire, inflicting pain and suffering upon the explosive juvenile. The small child is slapped for getting into mother's cosmetics, shouted at for bothering father with a dozen questions, whipped for jumping out of bed in the night to see what the grown-ups are doing in the living room. The older youngster is ridiculed for his daydreaming or his failure in school; he is ranted at for opening up his big mouth, soundly cuffed for sampling the contents of the liquor cabinet.

The exploring, experimenting needs of children, large and

small, are often inaccurately seen as disobedience, rather than what they are—the normal, if annoying, fulfillment of the child's developmental tasks. The power plays of the older child in his drive toward independence are especially subject to misunderstanding. His need to become his own man and interact with his peer group is frequently misperceived as selfishness and arrogance.

Children of every age need to test, question, and confront the older generation. It is a normal, universal exercise in the process of growing up. Just as the cutting of the umbilical cord at birth physically separates parent and child, there are social, emotional, and intellectual separations between the two throughout the remainder of the child's life. For many parents, this need of children to pull away stretches adult patience and control up to and beyond the breaking point. Mothers and fathers see the youngsters' behavior as defiant and disrespectful. They view the children as kids who are "just asking for it,"—and tne children get it. What they get is hit therapy.

When Mike picks on his younger brother or refuses to give a helping hand around the house, mother swings out at him to keep him in line. Whenever Sally back talks to her grandmother, plays hooky from school, or lies, she, too, FEELS her parents' wrath.

In many households where children's belligerence or laziness, contrariness or confusions, turn home-sweet-home into a discordant jungle, the law of the jungle rules supreme. MIGHT IS RIGHT.

> "Right or wrong, I just don't know what else to do with her except whip her," Betsy's mother confides guiltily to her neighbor. "She's my own flesh and blood, but that child drives me up a wall . . . and, when I've had it up to here, without even thinking, I hit her.
>
> "Heaven knows, I don't enjoy whacking her little

44

bottom, but I get so frustrated, so upset, I could . . . I'm certainly not a child abuser type," the mother adds quickly, "but like it says in the old cliché, even if it hurts me more than it hurts her, I've got to punish that child—for her own good. A four-year-old just can't be allowed to rule the whole family, right?"

The little dictator under discussion is a sullen preschooler. Whatever her leisure-time activity, it involves whining, complaining, and demanding attention. She butts into conversations, makes a nagging nuisance of herself, and reacts angrily whenever denied or ignored. Her father sometimes despairs that she just seems to have been born with a bad disposition.

Two older siblings somehow escaped whatever it is on the family tree that grew sour in Betsy. They are generally good natured, well-behaved children, rarely needing serious punishment. Their little sister's contrariness, tears, and temper tantrums, however, are so annoying to the family that she is the regular recipient of scoldings and spankings. "Right or wrong, I don't know what else to do," her mother admits, and she is right: She doesn't know any alternative.

The choice of hitting Betsy in order to knock some sense into her is a bad one. A better approach in disciplining angry, aggravating children is to get to the root of the problem. Like adults, children have to be both seen and heard. They have as much need to explode, ventilate, and exhibit their frustrations as they have to love and be loved. Angry feelings are normal and require tolerance. They are the smoke signals a child sends out to caution adults that something is wrong. When preschoolers resort to nagging and temper tantrums, they are crying for help. Spanking them only gives them more reason to cry; it enlarges rather than alleviates the cause for unhappiness and unacceptable behavior.

Hitting the misbehaving child of any age merely puts out the surface flare-up; it does not eliminate the fire. The youngsters' hurt and hostility still smolder, ready to erupt again at any time. Physical punishment temporarily frightens some children into discontinuing the particular action for which they have been hit, but it does not stop them from acting up in other, sometimes even more offensive ways. Children who are shouted at or slapped stay down only temporarily. Adults who practice hit therapy reap equally impermanent results for themselves. In the act of punishing the child, mothers and fathers feel justified and relieved; after their anger is spent, however, most are left feeling confused, contrite, or guilty. The sweet smell of success, initially experienced in subduing the misbehaving child, all too quickly leaves a bitter taste in the adults' mouths. After all is said and done, they, like the child, feel edgy and unfulfilled.

Regularly hitting, yelling at, and embarrassing a youngster offers no permanent relief for either the parent or the child. These methods do not get to the core of the problem. All the action is directed against the symptom, not the cause. The problem which triggered the misbehavior in the first place has been ignored.

To avoid the flare-ups which regularly occurred in Betsy's behavior, mother should have treated the cause, not the symptom. If the same amount of time had been spent investigating what ailed the daughter as was spent trying to eradicate the obnoxious warning signals she sent out, it would have been time well-spent. The procedure could have saved considerable wear and tear on both mother and daughter. Whatever it was that was gnawing at Betsy could have been uncovered—boredom, sibling rivalry, a need for playmates her own age, hyperactivity, or any of the many other physical, social, or emotional disturbances to which preschoolers are commonly susceptible.

When adults make an effort to acquire some basic knowledge about a child's behavior, they gain the wherewithal to get permanent results. Unlike instant rice or Instamatic cameras, however, instant knowledge is not readily available. It takes more time to diagnose than to prescribe. It requires time to learn what children are feeling and thinking—time to listen and try to understand before leaping on them.

"Time" in ample quantity and of sufficient quality is needed if parents are to find out why the child acts as he or she does. But time is a precious commodity. It is easier and quicker to rule with an iron hand than to handle a child with tender, loving care; for this reason many mothers and fathers find themselves fighting fire with fire. Upstarts are put down by ridicule, sarcasm, or slapping and whipping. Even when this method proves ineffective, adults keep using it, time and time again. They learn nothing from past mistakes. Nor do their children learn what the adults wanted them to learn in the first place . . . to behave.

Youngsters regularly punished by physical or phychological force don't learn to behave better. Nor do they learn to trust or respect their elders. Instead, they are taught to be suspicious, fearful, and disrespectful of those who should be nearest and dearest to them. Children who are repeatedly struck have no opportunity to acquire a role model of behavior most appropriate to *humane* human interaction. They learn, instead, to make war with their siblings, friends, and even their own parents. Most damaging of all, these youngsters are prevented from learning how to develop more acceptable alternative ways to express their anger, fear, or confusion. Most children who are hit learn only to try harder not to get caught, rather than to try harder to behave. Psychological and physical punishment of children is like a boomerang; it not only causes injury to the child who is its target, but also to many innocent bystanders along its field of force, and it usually comes back full circle to damage those who originally used it as their weapon.

The weapons Joan's parents used against her were ridicule, yelling, and slapping. Mrs. Evans, her teacher, could see their effects in Joan's activities at school. At nine years of age, she was already a bully, a sneak, and a tormentor. She constantly teased children, picking on them at their most tender point of vulnerability. Children who were short were called "Pipsqueak" or "Midget," chubby children, "Fatso," kids with glasses, "Four Eyes." Not once a day, but continually, the girl mumbled the offensive nicknames under her breath or wrote them on the board or in notes passed when the teacher wasn't looking. The targets of her abuse were frequently driven to tears, which only added to their shame and misery.

No matter what Joan did, she had an excuse for it. It wasn't her fault, she complained to the teacher, that other children got so close to her that they were bumped into or accidentally scratched. She couldn't help it if her feet kept stretching out into the aisle where they had no choice but to trip her classmates. She was the tallest girl in the class, and it wasn't her fault if her legs were that long.

The more children tried to steer clear of her, the more Joan gravitated toward them, poking, shoving, grabbing the dodge ball or hurling cruel and abusive words.

Joan's teacher was at her wit's end. If she were to report the hostile behavior to the home again, the child would be punished. But how? No doubt she would be screamed at, told how bad or stupid she was, and spanked.

"Just you let me know when she acts up in class, Mrs. Evans, and I promise you she won't be doing it for long," Joan's mother had loudly assured the teacher in front of all the other children one day. Joan had turned red and angry, but her mother continued, shaking a warning finger at her.

"We don't go for coddling kids in our house, isn't
that right young lady?"

Coddling kids, as defined by Joan's family, meant any kind
of disciplining other than screaming or spanking. In the
course of several discussions with Joan, the teacher had
learned about the "hit therapy" practiced on the youngster. If
the girl brought home a poor paper, she was ridiculed as stupid or lazy and reminded of how well her brother did in
school. Whenever she misbehaved, no matter how minor the
infraction, she was made to toe the mark. "What's the matter,
Joan? You don't know how to write up to ten?" she would be
asked when she forgot or wrote down incorrectly a telephone
number left for her parents. If she dropped a glass, she would
be ridiculed, "There you go again, Butterfingers! You're careful enough not to break your own things, but you're too
clumsy to keep the glass you're supposed to be drying from
dropping on the floor."
Not only shouting and sarcasm were directed at Joan, Mrs.
Evans learned, but many times the child was soundly spanked.
This punishment never left visible marks, but her teacher worried about the marks on Joan's psyche—the emotional scars.
These were reflected clearly in the girl's mistrust and mali-
ciousness. Just as Joan's mother and father demonstrated little respect for Joan's feelings, the child showed no respect for
the feelings of others. Just as they bullied her physically and
verbally, she vented her anger on those smaller and weaker
than she. Where would the vicious cycle end, the teacher wondered? How could she make Joan's parents understand what
they were doing to their child, to themselves, and to so many
others now a part of their daughter's life, including those who
would later become a part of it?
The "monkey see, monkey do" effect of hit therapy is its
most painful consequence. Hitting takes its toll sooner or later; the sins of the fathers and mothers who hit their children

49

are visited upon the children. Boys and girls like Joan frequently grow up to become men and women who lash out at others, not out of choice but out of choicelessness. Their own upbringing neglected to teach them any other way to deal with people. But long before these children mature to adulthood, they act out their fury and frustration on those around them—classmates, siblings, and, when they are big enough or brave enough, even on their own parents. They may torture pets or other animals. They may accidentally-on-purpose drop or destroy some possession valued by the person responsible for their hostility. Less courageous boys and girls constantly demand attention, become sick, act helpless and dependent—anything for revenge, anything to use what power they have against the men and women who strike out at them.

Although the dangers of resorting to "hit therapy" in disciplining children are real and ever present, it is certainly not unthinkable for a child to receive an occasional slap on the rear end. Nor need it be taboo for parents to amplify their voices in order to quiet down a noisy child. The age of the child, his offense, and the extent and degree to which such punishment is applied determine the usefulness, or abusiveness, of hitting. A quick swat to keep a three-year-old from running into the street does far less damage than allowing him to get run over. Shouting at a child who has appeared deaf to more reasonable ways of getting the message is better than never getting through to him at all.

What rarely gets through to children, however, is constant or unnecessarily forceful slapping or shouting. Overuse is not only abusive, it's useless. Such punishment becomes like water off a duck's back. Children who are regularly hit take their licks and lick their wounds, but it's the grown-ups who are all wet if they expect any positive or permanent behavioral changes in these youngsters. Children do not behave like angels merely because their parents knock the devil out of them. Quite the opposite: They become even more hellish to live with!

Sometimes, the resentment children feel when disciplined by hit therapy is directed, not against others, but against themselves. Children fail in school, abuse drugs and sex, lie, cheat, vandalize. They hit back at their parents by punishing themselves. They hurt the family and the family image by inflicting personal harm upon themselves. The verbally or bodily assailed youngster learns to become resentful, spiteful, and even more rebellious. Sooner or later, his misbehavior escalates in frequency and seriousness. Adults who know no response other than to hit are then left with little else to do but to keep hitting 'em again harder.

Many mothers, fathers, and other adults who live with children accidentally get caught in this revolving door of hostility. The vicious cycle may first be set in motion by the child's offensive action; it is then accelerated by a parent's unthinking use of punishment.

When Peggy spit at her little brother because he touched her photograph album, Mother slapped the girl. Ten minutes later, the little boy's fort of blocks came tumbling to the ground. Peggy was accused of knocking it down, but she denied doing it, insisting the blocks fell as a result of their own weight. Mother, still angry at the spitting incident, slapped the girl again, once for the offense and once more for good measure—for being untruthful. Incensed by her parent's failure to believe her, Peggy back talked the older woman.

Round and round the anger goes and where it will stop, nobody knows. The vicious cycle of "hit therapy" is not always caused by any actual offense on the child's part; sometimes it is a matter of a simple misunderstanding.

As ten-year-old Jerry hastily ran off for school, he thought he heard Mother call after him to tele-

51

phone her if he decided to come directly home from school that day. That way, she would be sure to be there so that he would not be alone in the house. It was Wednesday, a day when the youngster normally attended the Boy Scout meeting. What Jerry's mother had actually said was to call her if he wasn't coming directly home. The boy had been ill for a few days, and Mother thought he should skip the meeting and come home to rest. But, if he decided not to come home, she wanted him to call.

When Jerry failed to appear an hour after school had been dismissed, Mother became concerned. She called all over, the Boy Scout meeting, his best friend, his cousin, but Jerry was nowhere to be found. Actually, he was in the school yard playing ball.

By six o'clock, when Jerry finally got home, he got it—a barrage of screams and swats from a frantic, angry mother whose original message had failed to come through loud and clear.

Whether it is misbehavior or miscommunication which causes the conflict, neither person involved seems able to stop inflicting pain and suffering on the other. Had Mother established a clear-cut rule that Jerry always call home from wherever he is if he is not coming directly home, or if she had given the boy the message eyeball-to-eyeball, the situation, which turned out to be so uncomfortable for both parent and child, could have been avoided. If, upon seeing Jerry safe and sound, his mother had managed verbally to settle the misunderstanding rather than physically unsettling both of them, both participants would have been better off. Unfortunately, those who automatically resort to "hit therapy," for whatever reason, put themselves in danger of getting caught up in a momentum which takes control out of their hands.

* * *

Fourteen-year-old Bruce was a son who was difficult to handle. His mother blamed his father for being too hard on their son, for spanking and shouting at a boy his age whenever he misbehaved. The husband condemned his wife for coddling Bruce too much, making a Momma's boy out of him, making excuses for him. Whoever was at fault, Bruce was not an easy child to live with. He was disruptive at school, big-mouthed at home, a manchild too big for his britches as he confronted his awakening adolescence.

To state that Bruce was a problem would be to grossly understate the issue. He drank whenever he could, sometimes smoked pot, and hung out with the wrong crowd. Most of the values cherished by his parents—a good education, a good job, social responsibility—he ridiculed. His attitude toward school and his poor achievement record marked him as a youngster more likely to become a high school drop-out than a student at the college his father had attended.

The anger and resentment which the boy's attitude and actions generated in the father caused considerable friction between them. The day Bruce took five dollars from his father's desk drawer, the sparks really began to fly.

"You took it, didn't you?" the father screamed at the boy as he walked through the door. "The money from the desk, you took it, right?" The man's voice grew louder. With a careless shrug of his shoulders and a nod of his head, the son acknowledged the act and started to speak. He was cut short by his father's unleashed fury.

"You're nothing but a thief," the older man

yelled, as he landed one blow after another across the boy's rear end, back, face, and wherever else the flurry of his blows could reach. "We give you everything—food, clothing, money, love—and what do we get in return? A thief, a sneak, a liar," the father continued, completely out of control. "You took it! You took it—that's what you are, a taker, a taker, a leech, a drainer," he cried out as he continued to punish the boy.

Only when the screams of his wife, that he was "killing the boy," penetrated his anger—only when he heard her through his automated hitting and the son's loud sobbing—did the father stop suddenly—exhausted, confused, ashamed.

Bruce's shirt was torn where his father had grabbed him. His face was red and one arm was welted. What damage there was beneath his clothing remained to be seen.

The brash boy was now a weeping child, sobbing and screaming at the same time. "I'm not a thief; I didn't steal it, I took it. It was my allowance money for next week," he gasped for breath. "I'm not a thief! I needed some lunch money and you had already gone to work and I knew the money was there. It was mine, anyway, my allowance money. I'm not a liar," he sobbed.

Father stood mute and motionless. His eyes were glazed with pain and the terrible reality of what he had done and of what he might have done, had his wife's voice not stopped him. How could it be that he, an intelligent man, a reasonable man, an amiable man, could so completely lose control?

No, this was not the first time he had had to spank Bruce for some misbehavior, but he had never before beaten the boy—never before lost control of his senses. He had never before let out all his frustration and suspicion and anger so relentlessly and so ruthlessly.

It is easier to destroy a bridge than to build it; it is easier to start hitting a child than to stop. People succumb more quickly to loss of control when things get out of hand than to the maintenance of control. Any little spark of childish misbehavior or parental stress can cause an angry adult to combust: How a child looks, the attitude he projects, or his disrespectful or hasty words combine with the normal stress and strain of child rearing to generate trouble. That last straw, the one to break the camel's back, is a dangerous unknown.

Bruce's father was no more a tyrant or sadist than most other parents; he was a man who, in losing his temper, found a side of himself he never again wanted to unleash. When angry, the human being frequently resorts to his basic animalistic instinct—that of might being right. He gives little thought to the dire consequences that could result in exerting that might. Had Bruce's father been experienced in using a less explosive method of discipline than "hit therapy," the harm to him and to the boy might have been avoided. Had the man stopped and looked before he leaped on his son, the physical and psychological damage would not have resulted.

More serious than the welts or bruises on Bruce's body was the damage done to the boy's self-image. Father had told his son in no uncertain terms what he thought of him. LIAR, THIEF, TAKER, DRAINER. The angry words, like angry blows, left a painful imprint on Bruce's mind. He had been labeled an ingrate, worthless, despicable. Whether the evaluation was just or unjust, the boy was probably doomed to live up to his father's expectation of him.

The child who is told he is bad invariably proves it. He misbehaves for one of two reasons: Either out of revenge for being unfairly abused, or in response to his belief that he is really bad. Father told him so and father knows best. Whenever a youngster believes he is bad, he acts to fulfill the role written for him. The psychological dynamic occurring is called the self-fulfilling prophecy. A child acts in accordance with his self-image, an image that is molded in large part by how his parents express their picture of him. Mothers or fathers who convey to the offspring that he is stupid, ugly, or rotten rear a child who closely fits the description. In some strange, tragic way, fulfilling the adult's prophecy is the child's way of pleasing parents—of proving them right.

Phil was labeled a loser. He was a chip off the old blockhead, according to his mother. After her divorce from his father, she had tried to rear the eleven-year-old affectionately and effectively, but it was easier said than done. The boy was the image of his father, a man she deeply detested. Phil not only had his father's physical appearance, but his mannerisms, his speech habit, his slow, high-pitched voice. The boy's ears protruded from his head just like his father's, and he walked with the same slow, heavy step. Invariably, Phil suffered time and time again for being a carbon copy. He was constantly ridiculed about his effeminate voice, continually reminded of how much he was like his father, restless, selfish, lazy. Even when the boy walked on his tiptoes, it seemed to him, he was scolded for deafening the downstairs neighbors' ears with his damned elephant trampling—just like his father. Ridicule, sarcasm, and criticism were Phil's daily diet. Consciously or unconsciously, his mother made him pay the price for being his father's son.

As physical control of children is a brawn over brain method of discipline, so too is the verbal punishment of embarrassment or loud, abusive criticism. Words which sting the child emotionally hurt as much as the slaps which sting him physically. *If there is a difference between the two kinds of pain, it is that the pain of words is of longer duration.*

Whether by words or by wallops, children get hit below the belt whenever they rather than their unacceptable actions are attacked. A youngster is capable of changing his behavior in order to be accepted or to avoid being punished. He is unable to reshape his total being. When a child is labelled thief, liar, or selfish and lazy in comparison to a parent, he has no way to turn his total self inside out. By having the sum and substance of what he is judged unacceptable, the child is left totally without hope.

No youngster or adult should ever feel totally without hope, especially hope that the parent-child relationship can be fulfilling and enriching. But such hope does not lie in the use of hit therapy. Hit children are only left more hostile and more ready to repeat their objectionable actions. They are never exposed to ways of substituting acceptable behaviors for their offensive ones; adults are too busy hitting them to help them understand how and why different actions and attitudes are preferable.

Shouting at, slapping, and ridiculing youngsters applies heat, not light, to resolving misbehavior. In treating the symptom, not the cause of the problem, hit therapy never does more than give temporary relief to both parent and child. It puts out the behavioral flare-up, but it doesn't extinguish the child's fire. It permits adults to "get even," and to let off their own steam, but it leaves them feeling spent, confused, and often guilty.

Much of the adult guilt associated with the use of hit therapy is quite justified! Corporal punishment only trains the child to use physical violence himself. Without being provided a better model than the one employed by his mother and father, the youngster cannot grow to know and practice more sensitive and sensible methods for controlling behavior. Made to feel that growing up under the control of adults is more burden than blessing, he is deterred from developing a solid understanding of the need for both adult and self-discipline. Without this, it is doubtful that he can be trusted to control his own behavior when no one is watching.

The high correlation between abused children and parents who themselves were physically abused as children substantiates the fact that those who are hit, hit back, even if there are years in between the getting and the returning. A more immediate result is that children who are whipped and walloped are in serious danger of becoming emotionally beaten. They are taught to think of themselves as untrustworthy or undesirable. The consequences of this lowering of self-esteem are evident in the sense of powerlessness, anger, and fear characteristic of children with negative self-images. Their parents' evaluations are tragically self-fulfilling.

Verbal and physical punishment of children has a boomerang effect. It hurts those to whom it is applied as well as those who apply it. Parents cannot help but be hurt deeply when their children grow up not trusting them, not respecting them, not loving them. Men and women suffer a substantial blow to their pride when their offspring bring dishonor to the family; they feel cheated and unfulfilled when the children waste social and educational opportunities afforded them.

Because the opportunity to guide children knocks not once, but many times, parents have it within their power to make certain that punishing their offspring is not a hit or miss activity. By keeping their hands to themselves and their tongues in cheek, parents can hit it off well with their youngsters and feel better about themselves as parents.

4.

Killing With Kindness

In the children's story, *The Emperor's New Clothes,* only one small boy was candid enough to report the bare facts . . . that the Emperor was parading through the town without any clothes on!

The royal tailors had promised to make the ruler a magnificently beautiful wardrobe, but they had deceived him. They had never intended to sew one stitch! Instead, they had relied on their sales pitch to make him believe the lies that were being fabricated. So convinced was the Emperor of the tailors' sincerity and skill that when they pretended to fit him with the nonexistent new clothes, he immediately went among his people to let them see how grand he looked.

Some of the men and women gathered in the street were brainwashed by the fact that their Emperor *must* be wearing beautiful attire if he said so. Other subjects were fearful of telling their ruler what they actually saw. So all of the people joined together to compliment and praise his regal appearance. Only one small child in the admiring crowd cried out the truth. "Look, everybody, the Emperor has no clothes on!"

Because seeing was believing for the little boy, he was not fooled. Unfortunately, it is not so easy for parents to avoid being fooled. Were adults as capable of seeing the truth and telling it like it is to their children as was the lad who told it like it was to his Emperor, fewer youngsters would be adorned only in a halo.

Well-meaning mothers and fathers everywhere allow themselves to believe that their little angels can do no wrong. No matter what the children do, care is taken that they are not frustrated, held responsible, or punished. The youngsters are disciplined, or "undisciplined," by a method called halo therapy. What their parents consider to be the old-fashioned, repressive restraints of hitting 'em again harder have been replaced by a commitment to make the world of childhood all fun and games. After all, children are only children once. Why ruin it for them? Why not allow them to "enjoy, enjoy" their young years while they still have a chance? Soon, too soon, the bubble will burst; then there will be time enough for the offspring to be brought up to date about the real world.

Parental irresponsibility in the disciplining of children poses a real and present danger. Unless the purpose and the consequences of using one disciplinary method or another are fully understood, children will not be properly reared. The excessive whipping, shouting, and ridiculing associated with hit therapy invariably result in physical and psychological overkill. The other extreme, halo therapy, may be equally deadly. Can mothers and fathers "kill with kindness?"

To answer the question, we must investigate the degree to which constant catering or conforming to a child's will is good for him. Is never saying "no" to a child supportive, or does it pull the rug out from under him? Does the kind of adult behavior which puts the pleasures of children first rob grownups of *their right* to life, liberty, and the pursuit of happiness? Is it adult love or adult insecurity, indifference, or ineptitude that is responsible for parents giving in, giving out, or giving up to their offspring?

In the give-and-take of any human interaction, no one person can do all the giving while the other does all the taking. A successful partnership must be built on cooperation and mutual respect. Whether the participants are husband and wife or parent and child, there can be no strength in the union if one member is always the surrendering one. Each partner must appreciate and respect the wants and needs of the other, and both must understand that their individual wants and needs will often differ.

Human needs are the immediate or long-range requirements vital to physical and psychological survival. Food, clothing, shelter, rest, and exercise comprise some of the physical necessities of life. The need to be loved and to belong, the need for structure, the need for self-actualization are some of the emotional ones. Intellectually and spiritually, these are basic drives requiring satisfaction.

Wants are choices or wishes not absolutely crucial to healthy human functioning. Generally, they are desires associated more with short-range or immediate gratification. Johnny needs to know his father loves him. Even though the divorce between husband and wife has restricted the amount of time the boy sees his dad, Johnny needs affection and attention from him. Should the youngster feel rejected or unloved by this important adult in his life, his healthy emotional growth is impaired. Johnny also needs proper rest and proper nutrition in order to grow sound in body and mind. While Johnny may want what he needs, he doesn't always need what he wants. He wants a ten-speed bike, a new skateboard, and permission to stay up until midnight to watch the late movie. Denial of these desires will not adversely affect the boy's normal development.

Peggy needs to feel she is as worthy and valuable a person as her older brother who gets all A's in school. She also needs more physical exercise in order to burn off all the weight she has gained munching on junk food. She wants to see her brother fail a test sometime, wants to watch TV instead of read, wants to choose her own clothes. Although she often gets what she wants, she doesn't always need all that she gets.

Wants can be appropriate or inappropriate. They can be a part of the GIMME, GIMME or I WANT THAT AND THAT AND THAT, RIGHT NOW dynamic which reflects the child in everyone. Wants can be unlimited and insatiable, or they can be mature and prudent. They have their value in providing motivation and challenge which can result in personal or group achievement; nevertheless, wants need to be kept in proper perspective. Unlike needs, all wants do not need to be fulfilled. Children's healthy, happy development is best achieved when some of their desires are satisfied, some postponed, and others denied.

Mrs. Glass didn't believe in denying her little daughter anything. She and her husband had waited a long time before being able to have Penny. Both parents had gone through college, worked and saved enough to put a down-payment on a nice home in a nice neighborhood. Penny was no accident. She was planned for and wanted, and she was everything parents could want, a bright, beautiful five-year-old, who had already been taught at home to read, to write, and to play several songs on the piano. What Penny had never been taught was what the word "no" meant!

Seated inside her mother's grocery cart one day, the little girl decided she wanted a particularly large box of cookies she saw on the shelf. Patiently, her mother explained that there were already several boxes of cookies at home. Besides, it was too close to supper time for her to have any snacks. But Penny would not be denied. She insisted, pouted, and reached over toward the shelf, almost falling out of the seat to get the box. When that didn't work, she craftily started to cry at the top of her lungs, "I'm hungry! I'm hungry!"

As soon as the little girl's mother became aware that people in the supermarket were looking at her and at her beautiful, bright, pitiful little girl, she grabbed the big box of cookies and gave them to Penny. The crying stopped as suddenly as it had begun, as the now smiling little angel ripped open the cookie container.

Just then, a neighbor passing by stopped to chat. "Are you going to let her eat all of those?" she asked.

"No," Penny's mother replied, irritated, "just enough to get me out of here and get her home. Actually, she shouldn't be eating any cookies at all because it's so close to supper time . . . but what can I do?" her voice trailed off.

The neighbor laughed. "Well, you are BIGGER than she is," she replied, "so I guess you could take the box away from her."

Penny's mother looked oddly at her friend. "And take a chance on her screaming again?" she asked in disbelief. "No, thank you. Think of what people would think if they heard her crying . . . that I had probably just whacked her when nobody was looking or that I said something to frighten her to death. What kind of child abuser do you think they'd take me for if I walked blithely through the store shopping, while my own flesh and blood just kept on screaming she was hungry?" the mother asked.

Her neighbor nodded knowingly and turned away down the aisle. Within a moment or two, she turned back to remind Penny's mother about the importance of following Mr. Shakespeare's advice about "to thine own self be true," but mother and daughter were already at the far end of the store. It looked as if the little girl had already lost interest in the big box of cookies. Now she was clamoring for a large bottle of soda pop.

Whenever some people—including children—are given a finger, they try to devour the whole hand. Those in the habit of getting whatever they want, when they want it, develop insatiable appetites. When Penny's mother gave her the undeserved box of cookies, she was catering to the child's wants, not to her needs. The little girl was in no danger of starving, nor was it likely she would even suffer hunger pains were she to have been denied the snack. The only thing she really needed was to be told, "no." Whether the daughter yelled or yielded, Mother should have remained firm. More important than the avoidance of noise or the attitude of onlookers is a parent's own feeling that what she is doing is the right thing, both for her and for the child.

It was not right for Penny to fill up on cookies so close to supper time. It was not right for Mother to be forced into buying something she already had in good supply at home. Most importantly, it was not right to allow the child to get her own way by screaming. Having succeeded once, she would try, try again. Always giving in or giving up to children is wrong. It encourages them to try to do all the taking while expecting others to do all the giving. To give youngsters all the rights without any responsibilities is irresponsible child rearing. Saying what she meant and meaning what she said was the only correct thing for Mrs. Glass to have done.

But doing the correct thing with children is rarely the easy or popular thing. If it were, more mothers and fathers would be doing it! To have given Penny only one cookie, no cookie at all, or to have bought a small box of sweets and insisted she hold onto it until after mealtime would have been more difficult for Mother to do, but it would have been a better solution. While adult firmness doesn't always stop a child's screaming or misbehavior, it does show her the difference between acceptable and unacceptable behavior. It differentiates between her needs and her wants. A just, steadfast, friendly "no" in words or actions conveys loudly and clearly that the parent or teacher, not the child is in charge. Spoken fairly, firmly, and pleasantly, this kind of adult behavior is the kindest. It makes it possible for adults to stand up to children without having to knock them down. Unfortunately for both parent and child, Mrs. Glass did not stand tall. By stooping to the coercion of someone half her size, she not only shortchanged her offspring, but she diminished herself in the process.

Many adults find it difficult to stand up to crying, screaming preschoolers. When the little smarties pick the most crowded public places to wage their battles, parents quite often surrender without a fight. Mothers and fathers buy the expensive, unneeded toy or game in the crowded department store rather than bargain with a child's terrible temper tantrum. They promptly supply the cookies or soda pop from the shelf of the supermarket just to avoid the possibility of a bloodcurdling cry. They immediately provide the nickel or two for the bubble gum machine rather than face a torrent of tears. Faced with so seemingly cheap a price to pay for a little peace and quiet, the hand of mother, father, or grandparent automatically reaches for the nickel, the cookie box, the toy. It is a bad move!

Anytime grown-ups give in to a child when they should not, they become sitting ducks. The youngster quickly learns how to get a repeat performance every time he wants something. Time and time again, he is able to badger or bluff adults into capitulating because he has found the button which activates them. It is the panic button, a reaction device triggered by the pressure points of adult vulnerability to indecision, aggravation, or guilt. The youngster of any age who knows how to apply enough pressure is in a perfect position to push grown-ups around.

When parents continually conform to or cater to a child's will or wish, they provide wishy-washy guidance. Their method gives no support or structure to children because it has no fair, firm, consistent substance. Even when mothers and fathers, teachers, or other child caretakers realize the error of their ways, many continue to practice this way of child rearing. Some do it because they fear that the youngster will not love them if they put their foot down and say, "no." To be unloved is a human condition so intolerable, both in anticipation and realization, that parents are unwilling to take the risk. What few adults ever care to admit is that mothers and fathers need the love of their offspring as much as children need adult affection. It is natural and proper for parents to seek affection, attention, and affirmation from their children, but when they must satisfy their own need to be loved, *at any cost,* they pay a very high price.

It didn't take too much figuring out on Sammy's part to realize how much his mother needed his love. Recently, she had been divorced from his father, an arrangement not of her own choice. Her husband had found another woman—someone younger, sexier, brighter—she really didn't know, but a lover important enough to his life for him to give up his home, his son, and a large part of his salary in alimony.

At eleven years of age, Sammy was caught in the middle of his parents' separation. He loved his mother, and he loved his father. Even though they had both tried hard to make him understand that the divorce had nothing to do with him and that they both still loved him, the boy was confused and frustrated. He felt cheated and angry. Because he knew his mother needed him too much to fight back, Sammy took his anger out on her.

Not that he was deliberately cruel or disrespectful, but he demanded things! He demanded her time, her energy, her affection, her attention. Sammy never took "no" for an answer when he wanted anything. Whether it was clothes, money, or privileges not usually afforded a preadolescent, the son didn't have to take "no" for an answer once he realized the power he had.

He and Mother had been disagreeing about the advisability of his staying up until 12:00 P.M. on a school night to watch the end of a late movie. Mom had told him he would have to go to bed, movie or no movie. The boy replied that he wished Father were back home. Father understood him; that's why he loved him better than he loved her, Sammy badgered.

Almost as soon as his thoughtless words were spoken, the son was sorry. He had just said them because he was angry, not because they were really true. But when his mother started to cry and to tell the boy how much she needed his love, Sammy knew he had found the right button. It could be pushed at will to deliver whatever he wanted.

The need Sammy's mother had to be loved by her son is not unlike the need all parents have to feel loved and valued by their children. It is no different from the child's need for affection and attention from grown-ups. Virtually all human beings need to be needed. Although parents do not generally communicate their innermost feelings to children, as Sammy's mother did, most youngsters are smart enough to figure things out for themselves. They realize how vital it is for mother or father to experience the security and pride associated with being loved. When children understand the power of their love, both in giving it and in taking it away, they are in a position to make life a "trick" rather than a "treat" for adults. Some, like Sam, openly trick their parents. Others give them the silent treatment; they show by their lack of communication the absence of their respect and love.

In response, large numbers of mothers, fathers, grandparents, guardians, and teachers spend their lives bargaining with, bribing, or begging children for love. At all costs, they are determined to avoid having to say "no" to the child. These adults allow themselves to become little more than doormats and then are hurt and surprised when the children simply walk all over them.

Whenever people allow themselves to be used, they run the risk of being misused or abused. Mothers and fathers who know no other way to get their youngsters' love than by halo therapy may receive love, but the price is high and the product low-grade. The love they get is love without respect. Like a snowflake or a falling star, it is momentarily bright, but basically cold and impermanent. Such love lacks the substance and warmth necessary for a lasting relationship. It is solely dependent on what's in it for the child rather than on the kind of trust and dignity that should be shared by both age groups. Whenever the give-and-take of a relationship has the parent doing all the giving and the child doing all the taking, there is nothing at all of value in it for the adult.

Not only are the adults who continually give to children left empty-handed in such an interaction; the youngsters, too, are cheated. They are robbed of the firm and consistent structure all children require in order to develop into mature, self-disciplined individuals. Children denied sure, unintimidated adult guidance acquire no direction. They get lost in the maze of unlimited choices available to them. They grow into rootless, restless youngsters who search but never find their way in developing the sense of generosity and responsibility needed to live with other people. Their excess of freedom becomes more of a burden than a blessing.

* * *

Whenever Barbara's parents attempted to control any of her activities, she responded by insisting she had a right to be free, to be herself. One of the most overused phrases in her vocabulary, next to "ya know," was "my right." The fourteen-year-old never seemed to miss an opportunity to remind her parents of her right to privacy, her right to make her own decisions, her right to make her own mistakes. Barbara never talked about her responsibilities—only about her privileges. Nobody had acquainted her with the rights of parents. Mother and father had failed to teach her that parents had both the right and the responsibility to determine which rights were the right ones to be given to girls her age.

Barbara's parents were good-natured, well-meaning people who made rules only after the fact, not before. Their method of child rearing was one of reaction rather than action; they had no particular plan for guiding the child. They played it by ear. Much of the time they tried so hard to create a totally harmonious relationship with their daughter that they were naively deaf to the many warning signals she sent out.

"Okay, so you found out about Rich, Pat, and the other kids smoking pot and getting drunk, but that doesn't mean I do! What's the matter, DON'T YOU TRUST ME?" she asked innocently.

"What do you mean you can't understand where I got the money to buy the new blue jeans and sweaters in my closet? . . . I saved up my allowance. What? You can't see how I could have saved that much?—Well, ask me no questions and I'll tell you no lies," Barbara replied flippantly.

Not until the local department store detective

caught Barbara and a friend red-handed and red-faced walking out with several stolen sweaters hidden beneath their bulky coats did her parents start asking questions. The answers they got were not the ones they wanted to hear.

Their daughter belonged to a group of girls who shoplifted. Not that the young people needed what they stole. All were from families who gave the children not only all that they needed, but almost everything they wanted. The young people ripped off the store not for the sweaters or jewelry, but for kicks, for excitement, for something to do in their leisure time. They shoplifted in an unconscious search to test the boundaries of how far they could go. Because no limits had been set for them at home, they searched for limitation, for structure, for someone to say "no," outside of the home environment.

Children given too much, too soon—too many rights and not enough restrictions—are in danger of being killed with kindness. Halo therapy issues youngsters a license to speed into adult experiences without having first passed the tests for handling them. Children not yet big enough for their britches are foolishly allowed to wear the pants in the family. Ill-fit for the responsibility, they are forced to adapt as best they can. Some use sophisticated adult language as a means of "faking" the instant maturity bestowed upon them by permissive parents. Others attempt to cover up their inexperience by imitating the jadedness or cynicism they associate with adulthood. The youngsters are pressured into living up to adult expectations by playing parts for which they have received neither adequate rehearsal time nor skilled direction.

Like many men and women who direct children's lives, Barbara's parents confused supervision with "snoopervision." They walked on eggs, hesitating to overstep their bounds. So anxious were they to respect her right to privacy, they allowed her to isolate herself from their guidance. They confused independence with anarchy; they let her do her own thing, unaided and uncorrected by those older and wiser than she. Unwisely, some parents give in out of weariness; they are unable to see that their children have been taking them for a ride. It is a guilt trip, usually beginning with the hurt-filled voice of a girl like Barbara inquiring, "What's the matter, don't you TRUST ME?" The mere asking of such a question touches the rawest nerve of parental vulnerability. Not to trust one's own flesh and blood seems unthinkable! It is not only child-demeaning but self-debasing. Adults fully expect children to trust them. The possibility that mother or father would deny the same respect—or even the benefit of the doubt—to an offspring conjures up the kind of insensitivity with which few adults want to be associated.

To avoid or assuage the guilt, parents bend over backward to treat children like equals; some go so far that they fall flat on their backs. Even parents who know they know better than their children try to hide their qualified trust in them; they go along with what the kids say rather than following their own better judgment. Trust, like respect and dignity, symbolizes such an uplifting human condition that even parents who are down on their youngsters hesitate to put them down with an outspoken, "I'm going to trust my own decision in this matter, rather than yours."

Whether or not adults fully trust their children, most of them do trust their own memories. Often, this trust is misplaced. Looking back in their own childhood, many men and women see things through rose-colored glasses. Some blot out the rigid way in which they were actually reared because the memory is too painful. The scars of the hit therapy applied to them have been buried beneath years and years of repression. Other parents permissively pamper their offspring because they have not been able to forget their own feelings in childhood. Recalling the unfair or unsympathetic treatment they may have suffered at the hands of their mothers and fathers, these men and women fear doing unto their children as was done unto them. Instead, a pendulum effect characterizes their parental behavior and they give their children an overdose of what they fully believe to be tender, loving care.

Mistakenly, some parents equate parental love with absence of discipline. Perhaps they are compensating for their unpleasant memories of the disciplinary methods that were used on them. Perhaps, needing to repress their doubts about their *own* parents' love, they have conveniently forgotten that they, themselves, required or received discipline in childhood. In either event, the love-'em-and-leave-'em-alone method which these men and women use spells trouble rather than happiness for them as well as their children.

The grown-ups who have convinced themselves that, since they "grew up okay" without being regulated, their children will too, often fancy that discipline, like the color of one's eyes or the shape of one's nose, is genetically carried in some DNA molecule of human behavior. "They're good kids; they don't need anybody on their backs," are the comforting words with which these men and women deceive themselves. But, although children may not need anybody on their backs, they *do* need someone behind them. They need adults, strong and sure people, backing them up with the discipline they have not yet totally developed for themselves. The existence of just, firm, and consistent disciplining inside and outside of the home is critical if children are to become productive and responsible human beings.

No matter what real or imagined comparisons parents see between their own childhood and the way they are bringing up their children, comparisons are dangerous. Nothing ever remains the same. "Look, don't compare kids today with when you and I grew up," one father tells another. "Maybe it's television or the way everything is brought right out in the open, but whatever it is, they're smart—a lot smarter than we were," the parent announces in almost proud resignation.

"You can't put anything over on them or make them do what you want them to if they don't want to." Making children do what parents want them to do is not the rationale behind responsible discipline. The purpose of guiding children is to motivate them to do what they need to do and what they can be helped to want to do in order to mature into capable, confident adults. When children are left undisciplined, when they are allowed too much too soon, only a façade of maturity is constructed. Having no real substance, it is incapable of supporting the youngsters' healthy growth and development.

Alfred was a ten-year-old momma's boy whose demands knew no limits. He nagged for excessive attention, and griped and groaned as only a pampered self-pitier can do. His total dependency weighed heavily on his parents' patience, but they managed somehow to grin and bear his unbearable behavior. Many evenings, they could not leave the house because Alfred needed them around. Hesitant to stifle his substantial artistic creativity and skill, mother and father handled the boy with kid gloves. Fearful of frustrating his emotional growth, they accepted all of his unacceptable behavior. Unfortunately for both parent and child, they did not know how to accept the boy while rejecting his offensive actions.

Alfred's behavior was more a cry for help than a scream for attention. Down deep inside, he knew he needed limits. Wanting structure, the boy was irritated by his parents' failure to put their foot down and stand for something. He retaliated by demanding more and more of them—stretching the limits of their patience and their temper. Subconsciously, Alfred hoped to goad his parents into finally taking charge. He wanted them to give him the solid support of loving and leading he needed.

The real needs of children are never satisfied when parents

73

kill them with kindness. By allowing their son to lean on them, Alfred's parents were stunting his growth. They were infantilizing a boy who should have been growing bigger and better able to handle his own wants and needs. Mom and dad were also diminishing their own lives by cutting themselves off from being anything but their child's servants, catering to his will and whims.

When adults seek constantly to please a child at any cost, they may succeed on the surface, but at the expense of any lasting success. What Alfred needed was a dose of fair, firm, but friendly discipline. He needed to know, in no uncertain terms, that because mother and father diagnosed his behavior as unacceptable, they were prescribing an old reliable remedy. Perhaps their son would find it hard to swallow in the beginning, but it was for his own good. While his parents loved him, they did not like his behavior, nor did they enjoy being taken advantage of. They had the right to go out at night, to say "no," to expect support, encouragement, and guidance from him. From now on, the interchanging of affection, affirmation, and attention would be a two-way street. That he could no longer be the only one in the driver's seat was what Alfred needed to be told—frankly, calmly, and regularly.

As children grow and enlarge their own sphere of experience and power, adults have a drive to enlarge their own egos. Alfred's parents, although consciously bothered by his stifling dependence, subconsciously desired it. Such self-enlarging desire often underlies the tendency of many mothers and fathers to put their offspring on pedestals, elevating them far above their deserved position in life. Simply because children are their parents' own flesh and blood, some mothers and fathers idolize them. They view the offspring as an extension of the parental self. He or she is the hope and promise for the future, the second chance for adults to dream their dreams or achieve, through their progeny, the goals their own lives may have left unfulfilled. Under such circumstances, disapproval, even when it is warranted and necessary, becomes difficult for parents to express.

Offspring are seen as appendages of their creators. Whether the child grows to be a rich man, poor man, beggar man, thief, doctor, lawyer, merchant, chief, he is programmed to fulfill the great expectations of his parents.

"What handsome little men you have there," the passerby exclaimed to the beaming grandmother, out for a walk with her two grandsons.

"Oh, thank you so much," the older woman replied.

"How old are they?" the passerby continued.

Putting one hand on the head of the bigger boy and her other on the smaller one, grandmother responded with pride, "Daniel here, THE DOCTOR, is six years old. Frederick, OUR LAWYER, is four."

Neither Grandmother nor the passerby had any way of knowing whether Danny or Freddie were to be or not to be what was expected of them. But, either way, any time a halo is prematurely applied to a child, it is a bad fit. Too much pressure is put on the youngster to be the brightest and the best. Mothers and fathers, too, are caught in the bind of their own parental ego-trip.

When mother pushes her daughter into the career she wishes she had pursued, she forms a connection which often strangles both the offspring and herself. When father pressures his son into Little League, Pee Wee Football, and the Midget Hockey Team in an effort to have the boy grow to be the athlete he never became, he provides a shaky foundation for their relationship and for his son's self-image. Child abuse is practiced not only in bodily or verbal attacks on children. Youngsters are also damaged when they are fabricated into shadow people. In becoming surface projections of some other

75

self—the parental self—those growing up are diminished. Not only are they restrained from becoming their own people, exploring their own creativity and individuality, but they are denied the strength of adult support and structure.

Parents who must live through their children or for their children are not substantial enough themselves to mete out the discipline youngsters require. They not only show this, they know this, at least subconsciously. The knowledge does not bring them self-respect or peace of mind. To enlarge their own self-image, child-worshipping parents must bend continually to the child's will or whim rather than stand up to it. Once they begin, they are caught in a revolving door. Having put all their eggs in one basket, they are forced desperately to protect the investment they have in the child. They have no choice but to close their eyes to any fault. Even when they clearly see that their little bundle of joy is headed for a pack of trouble, those who practice halo therapy must continue to view their children through rose-colored glasses.

To see the child as he or she actually is, sometimes wrong, sometimes right, sometimes selfish, sometimes generous—a growing, groping, giving, and getting human entity—is beyond the capacity of many adults. Not only is the offspring not clearly in their sight, he or she is far beyond their reach. These parents are unable to communicate with their children freely and easily. They cannot enjoy them, interact with them, and maintain a relationship that is mutually satisfying. Moreover, elevating children to so high and mighty a position makes it difficult for parents to extend to them the discipline and support they need.

The extensive direction children require is not provided by oversolicitous, overprotective, or overanxious parents. Nor are youngsters reared wisely or well by mothers and fathers who practice halo therapy as a time-saving device. Unlike money, power, or beauty, human time is strictly limited and irreversible. It is the vital substance that parents must expend in order to direct, explain, guide, and communicate with children. It takes time to care and share, to give and take—time to be fair, firm, and consistent.

Many parents find that saying "yes" is a real time saver. It avoids the arguments, questions, anger, or disobedience that a restrictive "no" elicits. Adults who know little about the difference between a child's needs and wants become inveterate "yes" men and women. They know that saying "no" in order to limit or structure their youngsters' actions or attitudes would cut down on their own time. In having to listen, to analyze, to explain, to implement, many "leisure" hours would be unleisurely expended. So let the neighbor discipline the child if he or she acts up. Let the teacher spend the days trying to straighten out the boy's or girl's behavior. Project the guidance responsibility onto the school bus driver, the scout leader, the policeman, the social service agency, or even onto the child himself, but don't bother mother or father. They really don't have the time to say "no."

As the years of child rearing go by, it is the quality of the time rather than its quantity that makes for successful discipline. The amount of attention given to children depends upon the particular needs of the individual, child and adult alike. Whatever the quantity, the quality should not be flimsy. Halo therapy as a basic child rearing practice does not provide enough full-bodied interaction to support either parent or child. Children need boundaries upon which they can rely for their security and direction. Parents need the kind of love from the young which has respect and trust at its foundation. When children are killed with kindness, sooner or later the results are uncertainty, disrespect, and hostility among all concerned.

Children are in essence no more than children, sometimes angelic, sometimes devilish, but always wanting, needing, flesh and blood human beings. What they want and need is flesh and blood parents, not ghouls, goblins, or apparitions. Shadow people, the "yes" men and women who float in and out of children's lives, give them no support, but this is not because they have none to give. Nor is their behavior necessarily selfish or unintelligent. It has its roots in human emotions which are natural and universal—guilt, fear, and lack of self-esteem or competence. All people, to some degree, are burdened or controlled by these feelings, but adults who regularly succumb to them, adults who mishandle children by handling them with kid gloves, go too far.

A valid and reliable understanding of human growth and development supports several conclusions about emotions and behavior.

1. Adults have nothing to fear but fear itself when they are afraid that children will not love them, will defy them, or will be harmed creatively or emotionally by being disciplined.

2. Fair, firm, friendly, and consistent guidance does not rob offspring of the bliss of childhood, or their natural or given rights as children.

3. The appropriate expression of normal parental anger or displeasure is healthier for all parties concerned than grinning and bearing inappropriate child behavior. Adults need not feel uneasy or guilty when they stand up to children.

4. Living through or for children is an empty and dangerous pastime. Elevating offspring to a position way over their heads puts them out of reach of the enjoyment, support, and guidance they need to have from adults. It also puts the pleasure, respect, and trust men and women have a right to gain from children beyond their grasp.

5. Parents who mistrust their own adequacy or competence in knowing how to discipline children should remember that everyone is an amateur doing on-the-job training. Even professional child develop-

mentalists are amateurs when it comes to rearing their own children.

6. The difference between a child's needs and wants needs to be understood by both parent and child if discipline is to be administered wisely and well.

No child can grow to be self-disciplined unless he is parentally disciplined. Those growing up need a support system of parental concern and attention to serve as a model for their own adulthood. They need appropriate limitations and restraints to help them differentiate between their immediate and long-term needs and their desire for instant gratification. To mature into sensible, self-reliant, socially productive adulthood, youngsters need structure. This structure is not the repressive, constraining, put-down of hit therapy. Nor is it made up of the flimsy, wishy-washy paper tiger of halo therapy. Somewhere between these two unproductive methods of rearing youngsters is the sound, natural way—a back-to-balance therapy that is mutually satisfying to child and adult alike.

5.

FINDING THE BALANCE THAT IS JUST RIGHT

Jack Sprat could eat no fat;
His wife could eat no lean;
And so, betwixt them both, you see,
They licked the platter clean.

Somewhere betwixt and between the too lean guidance of halo therapy and the fathead formula of hit therapy, there is a balanced diet of discipline for growing boys and girls. It is an *all natural one,* containing neither artificial sweeteners or flavorings, nor harsh fillers and preservatives. This brand of discipline combines the best of the head and the heart. Both children and parents are able to thrive on it because it satisfies the needs of both.

The minimum daily requirements of emotional, intellectual, social, and spiritual nutrition for adults and children do not lend themselves to exact proportions. Individual boys and girls require different amounts of guidance at particular times.

How much discipline each parent is able to provide also varies. Whatever the balance of give-and-take between them, it rarely comes out fifty-fifty in any one instance.

Neither marriage, nor parenthood, nor even a business partnership is really a fifty-fifty proposition. On some occasions one participant may need to contribute 70 percent of the energy or time required to make the union work. At other times, that person may expect the other partner to supply most of the effort. Parents and teachers may find themselves at different times, either doing most of the giving or giving in to a child. Sometimes, it is the child who is expected to change the course he would like to follow in order to reach a satisfactory meeting of the ways with the adult. At different times and for a variety of reasons the give-and-take of energy, trust, and love between the partners in a relationship will change. In any one day, either child or adult may be doing more giving than getting.

No wholesome human relationship occurs when too rigid a balance is expected. No healthy, satisfying parent-child interaction results when one person determines he will give only "this much," and the other decides he will go only "so far" to make it work. Basic human needs churning inside of everyone constantly shape and change people. They affect their actions, attitudes, and expectations. How well mother feels one day, or how much financial stress dad is under, markedly affect the family give-and-take ratio. How secure sister feels socially, how much academic confidence brother has in himself, or how rejected grandmother feels, are only a few of the many determinants of human behavior on a daily basis. In the parent-child relationship, the mood and the motivation of the moment often dictate who will need to receive and who will need to give.

If one human factor is predominately responsible for throwing a family relationship out of kilter it is the adult's *inability to cope* with the elusively changing child. Not that parents don't give it all they have; most of them do. The problem results because growing youngsters function in a now-you-see-them now-you-don't fashion. They seem everywhere and nowhere at the same time; they are pushing, pressuring, exploring, antagonizing, demanding, defying, wanting, needing. Little wonder that few adults feel really secure about how to handle today's children. Exactly what is it children *need*? More discipline? Less discipline? More rights? Less responsibilities? Are children's needs different from adults' needs? When the needs of parents and those of children are at odds, how can their relationship be brought back into balance?

Achieving and maintaining a well-balanced relationship between any two people, day by day and year after year, is like participating in a complicated juggling act. Practice makes perfect only if the right technique is employed. No matter how many times the wrong thing (such as using discipline inappropriately) is repeated, nothing but imperfection results. In the act of juggling, concentration, keen-sightedness, patience, and skillful handling are the techniques required for keeping things in proper balance. Anytime a juggler loses touch with what he is trying to balance, he fails to keep his act together. Keeping the parent-child act together also requires skillful handling and keeping in touch. Both the needs of children and the needs of parents should be kept clearly in focus and upheld.

Jane barged into the office, sullen and scared. "I'm quitting college," she announced dramatically to the professor who was her advisor. "Maybe I'll come back sometime; maybe I won't! I just need to be what I want to be . . . my own person. . . ." The girl hesitated. "Could you sign this drop slip out of your course, please?" She jumbled the words together, emotionally.

"Why?" the professor asked simply. "You've done very well in college . . . good grades . . . you seem to get along with your classmates.

You're a senior now, isn't that right? In just seven more months you'll be graduating. You'll have your Bachelor's degree in business. Why quit now?"

"I'm NOT quitting," the girl responded sharply. "I just grew up, that's all . . . made up my own mind for a change. Twenty years of listening to what THEY wanted me to do, what THEY wanted me to be, and I woke up one day and said, 'No more.' Anyway, I'd rather not talk about it, if you don't mind. I've already gotten the big lecture about the tragic mistake I'm making throwing away my education . . . how selfish I am not to appreciate all that people have done for me all my life," she recited. "I just came in to say goodbye, and tell you I guess I won't be in your class this year."

The professor looked at the moist brown eyes blinking back the tears of frustration and confusion. The eyes said, "Stop me," although the lips said, "Let me go."

"I'll really miss you, Jane," Professor Brooks admitted honestly. "You've not only been a good and conscientious student, but I've enjoyed our discussions, and even our disagreements on life and life-styles. You've taught me a great deal I never knew."

The girl's eyes were perplexed now. "*I* taught YOU?" she inquired in disbelief. "The student teaches the professor? Don't put me on."

"It's true, Jane. The student did teach the teacher . . . perhaps not about the subject of 'Business Management,' but about the way your generation feels about things, about communication, about parenthood."

"Look, I really have to go," the girl answered nervously.

"Well, here's the signature you came for! Goodbye and good luck," the older woman offered as the student turned to leave. Then, the professor added softly, "Jane, I wish you could have found some other way to punish your parents—without hurting yourself."

The girl turned suddenly, eyes ablaze with anger and shock. "What do you mean, PUNISH?"

Professor Brooks' face reddened. It was probably not her place, none of her business, but she had said it. Now she owed Jane an explanation.

"Sit down, please, Jane. I know I have no right to interfere in your personal life, but being a woman, and a mother as well as a teacher, I, well, bear with me, will you? Coming from my generation, it may sound corny but, as your generation says, 'Give me a break.' You want to know what I meant when I said that I wished you could get even with your parents without destroying yourself. Maybe I can explain it if I can compare you with that beautiful green plant in the planter on my desk.

Jane looked quizzical.

"Not only is it a thing of beauty in and of itself," Professor Brooks continued, "but it's very special to me. There are a lot of plants around my office, but this one is special because someone special gave it to me. Once it was just a little snip of a cutting from the plant of a friend very dear to me," the older woman mused. "I must admit, that even in my most unnerving days, when students come in challenging me for a better grade, or when my faculty basket is filled with more term papers than I could ever hope to read, I get a lift when I glance over and see that beautiful living thing. I am pleased when its attractiveness becomes a conversation piece for visitors. What they are admiring is not only the plant, but me—the skill in my green thumb, as it were, to nurture a thing of such loveliness."

"I don't see the point of all this," Jane interrupted.

"Suppose that green bit of life came to understand how much I valued it," the professor continued. "Suppose, while we're supposing, that it felt angry with me for keeping it captive here on the desk—serving only my pleasure—rather than letting it grow free, out in the field in its natural environment. Suppose it felt I should be punished for my selfishness and possessiveness!"

Jane squirmed in her seat, but she listened.

"Since we've given the plant the ability to reason," Professor Brooks laughed, "Let's also give it the power of motion. What the frustrated plant might then do is topple itself off of my desk. In its desperate determination to escape and punish me, it wouldn't give a thought to its own fate."

Jane looked intently at the shapely spider plant.

"Corny as the comparison is," the older woman continued, "I think you get the message," She touched the younger woman's shoulder.

"If the plant uprooted itself merely to get even with me, of course, I'd be saddened. I'd miss the admiration of all the visitors who noticed it. I'd lose the plant's beauty filling this room. But the biggest loser of all would be the broken plant itself.

"Young people like you, Jane, are often nurtured by parents who need you to flourish not only for your sake, but to satisfy their own needs. Sometimes in the process, there is overwatering, overfeeding, overprotecting. Frequently, like plants, children are pruned too much or kept in one place too long. They are denied the opportunity to grow free, to get out into the sunlight of different, and perhaps, more beneficial exposures. . . . But isn't it a pity—such a waste of beauty—when plants or people can find no better way to escape their gardeners than by stunting their own growth, or ending it?"

Jane did not answer.

Later, in the many days and conversations that followed, the older woman and the younger one talked and shared. They grew to better understand the needs of grown-ups and of those growing up. With Professor Brooks' help, Jane came to realize why her parents were such task-masters. She began to understand why they drove her to "Achieve, Achieve." She learned why, whenever any decision about her life needed to be made, they put her through the mother or father knows best routine.

Jane was very disturbed to realize how many wasted years and wasted tears there had been between her and her parents. She had never really known them as people; they had not actually understood her. Her mother and dad had never seen her as anything other than their own property—to have and to hold onto, as they saw fit.

Perhaps Jane would never fully learn all the reasons behind her parents' need to control her life. Maybe she would have to wait until she had children of her own to come to grips with some of the subtleties of the parent-child relationship. What the young woman did realize, and for the first time, was that the actions of her parents were not malicious. They were merely misguided and mistaken.

Without realizing it, many men and women operate on misguided and mistaken notions. They rear their offspring without any plan, without rhyme or reason, without real understanding. Many do not recognize that the natural needs of children cause them to behave as they do. Neither are these parents aware of the degree to which their actions are motivated by needs of their own which demand satisfaction. Most adults believe that their behavior is selfless. They do what they do, convinced that what they do is motivated solely by their child's best interests. "Now you're going to take those piano lessons, like it or not. When you're a talented and popular young lady, then you'll thank me for what I did for you!" mother prophesies. To another child, father insists, "Don't think I slap you around all the time because I enjoy doing it; but you're just going to have to learn once and for all that I'm the boss around here! Lord knows what you'd turn out to be if I let YOU rule the roost. It's my responsibility to keep you in line even though hitting you hurts me more than it hurts you!"

Time and time again, both adults and the children they discipline are needlessly hurt because the needs of one or the other are misunderstood and/or unaddressed. Adults must be able, level-headedly, to differentiate their own needs from those of their children before they can establish any kind of balance between the two. Similarly, children should be helped to understand that parents are people in their own right. Men and women are not merely Howard's daddy or the lady who packs Ruthie's lunch. They are more than the car pooler, the allowance-giver, the chief cook and bottle washer. Parents are living, growing, needing human beings. But how can youngsters know this? Few adults ever bother to tell a child, honestly but inoffensively, that they, too, have needs. Not only rights, not only responsibilities, but needs! Much to their own disadvantage, many adults pretend that they are so big, so self-reliant, and so independent that they need nothing at all in the way of support from their offspring. But their game of *let's pretend* has no substance. Adults do need affirmation, affection, and appreciation, just as children do.

Jane's need to self-actualize involved more than her own self-image. She wanted an opportunity to become her own person, not only in her own eyes, but also in the eyes of her parents. She longed to be allowed to use her mind, express her feelings, and make choices. Mother and dad did not understand her need. Nor did they realize what she required from them to satisfy it. They were too involved in satisfying a need Jane didn't understand, *their own need for self-esteem.* Limited education had denied Jane's parents the opportunity to achieve the economic and social status which they believed represented self-worth. Hard working people of very modest means, they had put all their eggs in one basket—their daughter. They had designated her to become the star of the family; she would have to rise and shine where mother and father felt they had only faintly flickered. Whether she liked it or not, Jane had to graduate from college as a business major. This would enable her to earn plenty of money, mix with the right people, and really *be somebody.* But the somebody she had to be was a person who met her parents' needs, rather than her own.

What the girl's mother and father failed to understand was that in order for their daughter to be somebody in reality, she needed to have her own needs met. Like all children, she required the structure and the security provided by parental discipline. But that alone was not enough. She had to have a disciplinary structure flexible enough to accommodate her own requirements. Jane needed to be supported without being suffocated. She needed parental love and affection, but not the kind which demeaned her by infantilizing her.

Refusal to let a child grow up is practiced by many parents. Some retard the youngster's development by overprotection. They neglect to give him or her the responsibilities which foster self-discipline and self-reliance. They do everything for the child. They make excuses for his misbehavior.

"It's not really Vincent's fault he spoke so nastily to you: The poor boy hasn't been feeling too well lately," Granny apologizes. "Now it's not right to expect so much of Charlotte. We can't ask her to help set the table and dry the dishes too, when she has so much homework to do."

There is no excuse for parents who overprotect and make excuses for their children. By infantilizing those who need to grow up, mothers and fathers totally throw the youngsters' journey from childhood to adulthood off course. They set up roadblocks which keep the child from progressing through his normal social and emotional development. Young people of all ages should be given responsibilities. From the child expected to eat by himself or button his own shoes to the adolescent required to take out the trash or drive the car responsibly, children need to be held accountable for their actions and attitudes. Whatever tasks they can or should do ought to be carried out by them. Children permitted to be footloose and fancy-free at the expense of obligations never develop self-discipline. Given everything and required to give little in return, they never learn to wait for anything. Neither do they learn to compromise, to admit their mistakes, or to accept denial or defeat good naturedly and maturely. No child can grow to be socially responsible unless he is given early and continuous experience in assuming obligations.

To grow up sound in mind and body, young people should be exposed to increasing responsibilities in accordance with their age and their capability to fulfill the assignment. They should also be given increasing rights as well. Those given one without the other have no basis upon which to maintain their social and emotional equilibrium.

> "Just get it through your head, once and for all, that you and I are not equals, young man. I do the telling and you do the doing. You're not old enough to have any choices. I'm the one who makes the decisions around here, and it doesn't matter WHAT you think, understand? I make the rules; you follow them. End of conversation."

> "Now, look here! Just you keep that mouth of yours shut. That's what people mean when they say kids should be seen and not heard. You're not even dry behind the ears yet. Who gave you the right to say one word about this?"

* * *

The rights of free speech, free thought, and free choice are normally desired by all human beings. They are rights which should be extended to children. When children are seen and not heard, they are hurt. They are denied needed experience in speaking more clearly and coherently. They are deprived of the practice of thinking logically and choosing wisely. When young people of any age are encouraged to exercise their rights, they develop feelings of self-worth and confidence. They feel they matter; they feel trusted and respected; they more readily learn to respect and trust others.

Adults, too, benefit from taking time to listen to children. They put themselves in a better position to guide boys and girls by learning all three sides of their behavioral story—the child's side, the other side, and the truth. Only when adults look at a situation from all sides can they make sound judgments about the responsible thing for them to do, or the right thing to say in each parent-child interaction.

"Fine, Dianne, we're glad you told us how you feel . . . and we can understand how you might get insulted when Dad reads the paper or when I continue cooking, when you want our undivided attention on a composition paper you've brought home or a diorama you've made for social studies class. That's something we're going to try to remember. What you might want to remember from this is that we also get angry when people don't pay attention to us. Just because we're adults doesn't mean we're old fossils who've turned into stone. Parents have feelings just like you do. We need to feel people care about and pay attention to us, too."

"Look, Glenn, there's no school today because of the snow. I can just see by the look in your eye that you're raring to go and in the mood to jump around and get into things. I have a lot of work to do and I can't be disturbed with noise or worrying whether you're going to knock into something and break it. Do you understand? Now here's the choice you have: You can either bundle up and go outside and make all the noise you want, or you can stay inside and play quietly. Either way, both of us can get along with each other."

When parent and child understand and accommodate themselves, not only to their own moods and motivations, but also to those of each other, they are in the best position to reach a balanced relationship. Talking about and finding compromises where each partner gives up a little for the common good is one good way to start. Everybody feels better if he can win a little and lose a little, rather than having to chance a tug of war which can only end with winner take all.

"Look, John, please keep that stereo volume down while I'm trying to concentrate on this work I brought home from the office, will ya? Tonight, when you're doing your thing with your friends on the telephone, I'll return the courtesy by taking the carpentry work I have to do out to the garage so as not to disturb you."

"Today, honey, you are going to have to eat the peas because Mommy already cooked them, and we can't let them go to waste. Tomorrow, it will be your turn to choose whatever green vegetable you'd like to eat."

Suggesting alternative or more acceptable ways in which children's needs can be gratified is very effective. By using this method, parents help youngsters learn how people use their minds as well as their mouths in trying to secure their requirements.

* * *

"Dad says it's impossible for you to borrow the car tonight, but he'll be happy to give you and your friends a lift to the bus."

"You cannot jump on the living room sofa, but you may jump all you want in the sand box outside."

"No, we can't let you have a sleepover pajama party for fifteen girls, but I think, for just one night, the house might accommodate your inviting six or seven friends."

Frequently, it is the number, place, time, or people involved which causes adults to legitimately deny the pursuit of happiness which the child has mapped out. Part of the youngster's plan may well be acceptable, but the good goes down with the bad if mom and dad pounce before they ponder.

Sometimes a flat "no" is the only answer that can be given to a child. More often than not, however, there need be no total winner and no complete loser in the battle of will and wit between the generations. Discussing problems together, pointing out to the child the aspect of his behavior that is unacceptable and suggesting and eliciting ways in which differences of opinion may be worked out is the most solid way to strengthen the bond between parent and child. Whenever men and women take the time to help their youngsters shape an unacceptable behavior or intention into a permissible one, they find that in almost no time at all, a more secure and satisfying relationship is achieved.

Had Jane's parents made the effort to recognize and help their daughter satisfy her own needs, both Jane and her parents would have grown together rather than apart. Had they listened to her, encouraged her ideas, and allowed her to choose the little things—her own clothes, books, friends, and interests—their daughter would have felt less repressed and resentful. She might have been more ready and willing to take their advice in the bigger decisions, such as which course of study she should follow in college. Had the girl been allowed to make many of the less critical choices throughout her childhood, the young woman's desire for self-actualization would have been better met. Such enriching and necessary responsibility would have resulted in her acquiring skills and knowledge more valuable even than those represented by her endangered sheepskin. Jane would have learned much earlier to respect and trust her parents. She would have felt more stable and confident as a person, knowing they trusted her and valued her opinions. The young woman also would have gained crucial experience in wise decision making. Certainly, she would have made some unwise choices along the way, but even her errors could have helped her mature in her judgments and selections.

One of the best ways for children to learn to look before they leap is to be allowed occasionally to take the plunge. Once a youngster has decided to waste his allowance on a worthless trinket, or to continuously court the friendship of a peer who delights in hurting him, or to leave a job that must be done until the last minute, he should be left to make his own mistakes. Poor decisions are the stumbling blocks which become the stepping stones to better choices. Children learn through wrongdoing as well as through doing right. As long as the options given to the child are ones which he can handle . . . as long as any choice he is allowed to make will not cause permanent or serious damage to himself or anyone else . . . a youngster needs to be free to make the wrong choices. Mistakes help boys and girls develop a perspective from which to view the options and the consequences of their next effort at decision making.

Jane's decision to quit college was little more than an adolescent spurt of anger and vengefulness. It was neither logical nor worthy of her. The haste that might easily have made waste in her life resulted from an imbalanced parent-child relationship of long duration, one in which a basic need of the girl's remained unsatisfied. Had the young woman not felt that her parents had made every single decision in her life, her dissatisfaction would not have been so deep, or so potentially destructive. Fortunately, the intervention of Professor Brooks kept a young woman sorely lacking in good decision-making experience from deciding to cut off her nose to spite her face.

In the one semester before Jane graduated from college, she learned more than many people learn in a lifetime. She learned that both adults and children are disciplined by the same internal structures. These internal disciplinarians are called basic human needs. They are the physical, social, emotional, and intellectual drives churning inside of everyone. In an effort to satisfy his or her needs, one human being frequently comes into conflict with the needs of others. The child attempting to satisfy his need may clash with the parent trying to satisfy his or hers. The youngster may shout, squirm, push, pull, and make a head-splitting nuisance of himself. What he is really trying to do is to see, hear, taste, smell, and touch the physical world around him. At the same time, the adult's energy level, attention span, or noise level tolerance may neither be a mix nor a match with the child's.

Whether parent and child are attempting to gratify similar needs or working on entirely separate ones, one is bound sometimes to rub the other the wrong way. The friction created frequently generates more heat than light. When the energy needed by both for enrichment and enjoyment of life is wasted in getting all steamed up, love, trust, and respect between child and adult diminish, and the basic needs which motivate human behavior fail to develop a happy, healthy parent-child relationship.

These are some of the specific principles upon which this balance depends.

1. The way an adult or child acts is largely motivated by that individual's response to basic needs. These internal dynamics affect and change the way people behave, what they say and think, and what expecta-

95

tions they have. Neither grown-ups nor children deliberately plan to make life miserable for each other.

2. It is perfectly natural for the needs of children and the needs of parent to conflict. No wholesome human interaction is static or perfectly balanced. The give-and-take ratio between adult and child depends upon specific and changeable moods and motivations. Sometimes one and sometimes the other has to give more than he or she gets. The balancing of mutual needs requires that both parties be able to give without feeling taken, and take without suffering guilt.

3. The most delicate balance in the parent-child relationship exists between rights and responsibilities. Like adults, children of all ages need both. They should have the right to exercise freedom of speech, thought, and choice. They should be allowed the responsibility of handling whatever rights they are accorded whenever possible. Both the kind and the extent of a youngster's opportunities and obligations should come as a result of agreement between child and adult.

4. Children given the right and the responsibility to make many small choices for themselves gain needed skill in wise decision making for the more important judgments which will come. They are also more likely to allow their parents to participate in some of the bigger decisions ahead.

5. Giving children their say does not mean giving them their way. Parents are people, too. They have needs requiring satisfaction just as youngsters do. Moreover, mothers and fathers are older, and in most cases (although not in every case) wiser. It is their privilege and their duty to have the last word—a word which, if it is uttered fairly, firmly, and consistently, will provide the kind of balanced discipline that is JUST RIGHT for everyone.

6.

BASIC NEEDS AND HOW TO MEET THEM

In the story "Goldilocks and the Three Bears," the little blonde intruder persistently tried and tried until she got things just right. First she tried Father Bear's porridge, but it was too hot. Next, she tried Mother Bear's porridge, but it was too cold. Finally, she tasted Baby Bear's porridge, and it was just right—so she ate it all up.

Not only the breakfasts, but the chairs and the beds belonging to each of the three bears underwent similar testing in Goldilocks' search for personal satisfaction. The trial-and-error method used by the little storybook character is the same one real children use. Youngsters of all ages try one thing and then another until their individual needs for nourishment and comfort are met. They spend their lives seeking and sampling in an effort to satisfy basic needs.

All human beings have the same requirements: Someone to love them, something to do, and something to look forward to. Psychologist A. H. Maslow more fully described these forces which motivate human behavior by subdividing them into five categories: Love and belonging, esteem, self-actualization, physiological gratification, and safety. Together, they are primarily responsible for causing those growing up and those who are already adults to act and react in the ways they do. When needs are satisfied, either temporarily or more permanently, a person can direct his energy toward enlarged activities and interests. When needs are unmet, stress and strain result. This pressure proves so distracting that it impedes concentration upon aspects of life above and beyond the unsatisfied need. The malnourished, hungry child puts little energy into building friendships with his classmates or learning to read. His biological need is all-encompassing. The child who feels that his working mother doesn't give him enough attention or affection is likely to hold on tenaciously to a teacher or baby-sitter. On the other hand, he may react to the stress of his unsatisfied need to belong by eating obsessively or misbehaving excessively. What the child tries to do, one way or the other, is to gain a substitute satisfaction for his particular need. Biologically or behaviorally, he looks for ways to compensate for the inadequacy of mother's love.

The psychological "wear and tear" of unresolved needs erodes confidence and causes physical and emotional discomfort. The toll on children is particularly harsh. They are much more limited than adults in the options they have available for gratifying their drives. They lack experience to handle maturely the frustration which results. The younger or more inexperienced a child is, the less he possesses the social or emotional security required to sublimate or rationalize his discomfort away. In sheer self-defense, children have to do something quickly to gain relief. Unable to get what they want one way, they try something else—almost anything else. Frequently, they do not stop to think through the consequences of their action. This immature hastiness is what gets them into trouble. Much of children's misbehavior is caused by their misguided effort to relieve the stress of unresolved needs.

Not only the will to gratify basic needs, but the way these needs are pursued, is an integral part of human nature. The five needs associated with growth and development are not a collection of unrelated mechanisms. They form an integrated whole which determines how people act. Furthermore, there is, according to Maslow's research, a sequential order in which each need component should be effectively met. Human needs form a specific hierarchy of importance. Adults familiar with the operation of this "need ladder" are one giant-step ahead in successfully disciplining children.

Administering fair, firm, and consistent discipline requires a knowledge of some basic principles of child development.

1. Children's attitudes and actions usually have understandable causes.

2. The way in which children behave is largely determined by their maturational level and the patterns they have developed for satisfying their needs.

3. When parents treat the cause rather than the symptom of a youngster's misbehavior, they contribute to a parent-child relationship rewarding to everyone.

When a child behaves stubbornly, disrespectfully, or disobediently, many mothers and fathers look upon the outburst as deliberate defiance. Their normal reaction is to fight fire with fire. "He's not going to get the best of me by getting away with this." Most parents respond only to the child's offending act rather than to his needs. Few parents take the time to ask: "What does Sally require to make her less anxious and less antagonistic?" "What is it Scott is really trying to tell me by acting up this way?"

Every day, in a variety of ways, boys and girls attempt to tell the adults in their lives something. In so doing, few choose arbitrarily to act exactly as they do. Their behavior is largely determined by the need within them. Boys and girls are all wound up in their cycle of need satisfaction. They seek physical well-being, self-worth, and intellectual growth. What they seek, they manage to find, one way or another.

"I don't know if there's another child like her, I swear," the mother of two-and-a-half-year-old Annie complains exhaustedly to her husband the second he walks inside the door. "Here, you take her; I've had it . . . up to here!"

"What's the matter?" the little girl's father asks innocently.

"The MATTER . . . well, I know she's my own flesh and blood . . . and that a mother's supposed to love her own child . . . but, sometimes, Gordon, I'll tell you the truth . . . all her squirming and ransacking just plain gets on my nerves! . . . Sometimes . . . here all alone with her all day, without hearing any adult voice besides my own . . . it's all I can do to control my temper. I . . . I don't know where the devil she finds all her energy, but . . . one thing's for sure . . . she knows just how to make me lose mine. . . ."

"I felt it was only fair to tell you," the third grade teacher reported grimly to Dan's mother, "that the reason your son never gets his work done in class . . . is because . . . because . . . ah . . . he's too busy . . . playing with himself. Everytime I look at him, there he is, touching and rubbing . . . now, I know this is embarrassing for all of us, Mrs. Marshall," she continued hastily, "but we just cannot permit him to do that sort of thing in school. The other children will begin to see, and then what? I've called you in to see me because I think you ought to tell your husband to talk to the boy about it immediately."

"There seems no immediate need to run Fred

through any more tests." Dr. Baker advised. There's no enlargement of the glands in his neck . . . so I doubt that he has mononucleosis . . . I'd say that the reason your son acts so lethargic all the time . . . as physically limp as a dead fish . . . as your husband described him to me, Mrs. Mansing, is because Fred is just a normal adolescent. To label him lazy and irresponsible, as Mr. Mansing did on the phone yesterday, really isn't fair. Your son is undergoing significant hormonal changes. You could say he's growing up inside and out. That's what this stage called adolescence is all about."

"But, Doctor, he really is just like a . . . well, like my husband said, limp and useless around the house."

"I'm sure it seems that way to you." Dr. Baker agreed. "The energy a fourteen-year-old boy's body needs for all the growing it must do saps his strength. It's not easy for adolescents always to be alert, have pep, or concentrate on their responsibilities as well as we might like them to."

"You're sure he's not sick or stubborn, or anything? It's just . . . normal . . . for him to act so disinterested and exhausted all the time?"

"Yes," the Doctor replied. "Just try to bear with him. Accept him as he is, see that he gets plenty of sleep, and if you can, try to talk him into putting better nourishment inside his body than the junk food most kids his age eat. . . . That ought to take care of him."

Taking care of physiological needs is the first and foremost priority in the human need ladder. Two-and-a-half-year-old Annie's hyperactive preoccupation with seeing, hearing, tasting, touching, and examining the world around her, Dan's exploratory investigation of his own bodily parts, and Fred's adolescent energy slump are natural, normal manifestations of the biological drives within them. Two-and-a-half-year-old Annie's getting into everything here, there, and everywhere (including her mother's hair) was not calculated to exhaust her mother. The preschooler's purpose was merely to educate herself about her environment. Eight-year-old Dan's masturbation also represented little more than a small boy doing what comes naturally. His activity was not meant to upset the teacher, lead his classmates into evil ways, or embarrass his parents. Such ulterior motives rested, and caused unrest, only in the minds of the adults who misunderstood the boy's actions. Similarly, teenage Fred's "limp as a dead fish" posture was not meant to bait his father or absolve the boy from doing work around the house. Few children of any age deliberately or maliciously set out to drive their parents up a wall. If a wall exists between adult and child, its construction is frequently the result of adult misinterpretation of the motives behind the boy's or girl's behavior.

"That kid can't kid me. Marcy's not as dumb in math as she pretends to be," Mother charges emphatically. "She's just lazy. If she really put her mind to getting better grades in school, she could."

"Richie knew damn well I needed his help cleaning out all the winter junk in the garage this weekend. Why else do you think he suddenly volunteered to help his gym teacher set up batting practice for the Little League team over at the school!" Father grumbles.

It is not unusual for parents to view the activities or attitudes of a child through adult eyes. Unable or unwilling to recognize the role need satisfaction plays in shaping a youngster's behavior, some mothers and fathers misread into the child's actions a kind of adult cunning or cynicism which is

102

not actually there. Adults fail to see that the cause-and-effect relationships they formulate are not always the same ones upon which the younger generation operates. Such misunderstanding causes parents to ridicule, punish, or even seek professional help for their offspring, when none of these measures is warranted. Children are penalized for innocently doing what seems appropriate to them. They become confused and angry when adults jump to conclusions and then jump on them. Many youngsters respond by continuing to do whatever it is the adults insist that they stop doing. Either because they know of no other way to act, or as a way of getting back at the unfairness of their adult antagonists, boys and girls continue to be unlovable and consequently, unloved.

"... so, just let them keep on tearing into me; I can take it. And I can give plenty back, too. They're not going to flatten me into some kind of clone of them . . . liking what they like, doing what they do, being like they are. . . . Why is it so hard for them to understand that I'm my own person . . . with my own feelings and ideas and things I have to do? Why is it they think everything I do is bad or wrong?"

Whenever the normal or necessary maturational responses of a child are mislabeled as disruptive, malicious, or deviant behavior, a vicious cycle is begun. Parents set their sights on punishment rather than on trying to gain insight into the causal factors. Children seek to avoid contact with their mothers and fathers rather than achieve it. Not only the parent-child relationship but the entire emotional and social growth of young people is stunted when adults fail to understand and accommodate the need-seeking behavior of children.

No matter what satisfaction the child is pursuing—physical, self-esteem, safety—it is that one which tends to monopo-

103

lize his effort and energy. Until certain crucial needs are gratified, they preoccupy his thoughts and actions. Boys and girls seem unable to fully concentrate on less demanding drives such as getting good grades in school or fulfilling home chores, no matter how much external pressure adults exert on them. Professor Maslow calls this sequential handling of human needs "the hierarchy of prepotency." Less potent needs are often minimized, forgotten, or even denied by the child whose more basic needs are unresolved.

The needs which motivate human beings, from the most basic level to the least demanding, are:

PHYSIOLOGICAL SATISFACTION
SAFETY
LOVE AND BELONGING
ESTEEM
SELF-ACTUALIZATION

1. PHYSIOLOGICAL NEEDS consist of those conscious and subconscious capacities relating to self preservation and the sex drive. Both children and adults have nutritional needs, sleep and relaxation requirements, and energy and attention-span levels. Behavior is also governed by other biological functions, such as excreting, breathing, and satisfying sexual drives. Although the basic needs of parent and child are exactly the same, the methods used to fulfill them and the degree to which one need or another shapes the person's behavior differ. From birth through adolescence, children are more likely to give greater time and attention to meeting physiological needs than adults do. Whatever the biological necessity, each and every one that operates in boys and girls becomes a force which shapes and changes their behavior. The reactions of mothers, fathers, and teachers to these behaviors set the stage for either a cooperative or a combatant relationship. Penning in the exploring three-year-old, restricting the second grader from going to the bathroom except at specific times convenient for the teacher, or punishing the insatiably hungry teen-

ager for the trips he makes to the refrigerator, put blame where it is not due—on the child. However unintentionally, parents are at fault when they make demands upon their child which run contrary to his or her physiological needs. Adults who prematurely force toilet training on the preschooler or who rigidly avoid discussing sex or alcohol with the inquisitive preadolescent set up roadblocks in their child's path to normal development. Parents who demand unreasonable, prolonged quiet, immobility, or attention from children, or those who suspiciously try to interfere with the human sexual drives of the adolescent as expressed by his desire for privacy with respect to mail, telephone conversation, and social interaction get in the child's way. Unnerving and unnecessary discipline problems are created when adults are unaware of or unwilling to accommodate themselves to the fundamental human requirements of their children.

Understanding, accepting, and accommodating oneself to the physiological needs of children does not mean giving in to whatever means young people choose to satisfy them. Toddlers who need to exercise their muscles and their minds by crawling, examining, and jumping need not be allowed to perform on the living-room table. Nor should they be permitted to engage in their clatter when dad has a splitting headache or when company is calling. Similarly, the older child's urge to find out what amount of intoxicants his body can "hold," or how well he can measure up to the sexual expectations of his peers, need not be allowed unlimited expression. There is a proper time and place for almost everything. Children should be guided to understand and obey this law of coexistence.

"We seem to have reached the point of no return with our nine-year-old son. He is making our family mealtimes miserable. Either he has ants in his pants, bees in his bonnet, or something, the way he just cannot sit still at the dinner table. He fidgets and squirms, taps his feet, and leans all over on his elbows. Recently, he has been insisting he needs to be excused to go to the bathroom. It takes him so long to return to the table, his food is ice cold.

Now his father refuses to give him permission to move from the table until we're all finished. Billy just sits there with a pained expression on his face. He makes me feel more uncomfortable than he probably is. My husband says the only way to straighten our son out is to let him feel something a lot harder than the chair seat against his bottom if he keeps complaining at dinnertime."

Preadolescent boys are made of snakes and snails and puppy dog's tails. Their perfectly normal hyperactivity results in a lot of acting up. Not until the time comes when they grow big enough to get their act together do many of them develop the self-control parents prefer. Billy's real or imagined need to go to the bathroom is a situation which needs investigating. Perhaps he is suffering from a bladder infection. Maybe he feels so emotionally tense at the table that his biological defenses have mobilized to rescue him from that environment. Possibly he's full of junk food, eaten too close to dinnertime, or he is "turned off" from eating at mealtime by the large amounts of food put on his plate. Whatever the cause, it needs to be known before his parents can intelligently respond to the symptom.

One way to gain insight into the cause of a child's behavior is merely to ask him. Two words of warning, however, should precede the use of this approach.

1. Question him either an hour or two before you anticipate his squirming and complaining will take place, or about the same amount of time afterward.

2. Provide him with one or two possible reasons for his problem. Offer these in a casual not a judgmental way.

"Could it be your anxiousness to watch television which makes you in such a rush to leave the dinner table?

106

"Maybe you would squirm less if you tried to go to the bathroom directly before you come to supper. What do you think?"

When adults quiz a child in the heat of his misbehavior, they usually come up with the wrong answers. The youngster is too threatened or insecure at the time to concentrate fully on his problem. Even if he does know its cause, he is rarely able to put his feelings into words at that moment. Parents who help their child verbalize his emotions by suggesting some plausible reasons for his actions, open the door to his sharing the basis of his behavior.

Some children are not able, even with help, to zero in on what is bothering them. If a parent is unable to diagnose the cause of a child's mealtime miseries this approach may be tried.

Get the boy to agree that he will be responsible for making sure that he does not eat anything at least one hour before dinnertime. Insist that he also be responsible for regularly going to the bathroom, immediately before sitting down to supper. Until he adjusts to this scheduling, encourage the family to wait a few minutes before beginning the meal. Tell Billy, in advance, that he will be expected to sit and eat with the family until the supper is completed. Try to include him in the family table talk. This will center his attention on using his ears and mouth rather than his arms, legs, and body. He will receive more complete nourishment that way, too . . . both food for the body and food for thought.

"I thought I told you never to let me catch you touching a cigarette," Dad shouted angrily at his twelve-year-old daughter. "Don't you have a BRAIN in that head of yours? It's too late for me to stop, but damn if I'm going to sit still and let you get hooked on that weed," he growled. Grabbing the cigarette from her fingers, he pushed his daughter down roughly into the chair.

107

* * *

Whatever is said or done to children, might never makes right. Whether it is thumb-sucking, staying in bed when put there, hyperactive or lethargic behavior—or any other experience through which children are exploring, experimenting, or expressing their biological urges—a child's needs should not be ignored. They should be respected. Failure on the part of parents or teachers to recognize and comply with the basic requirements of those growing up results in miscommunication, mistrust, and misbehavior. Boys and girls are forced to feel guilty and insecure, even when engaging in behavior perfectly normal for their age or maturational level. Denied success in exercising their basic physiological needs, children are restrained from smoothly progressing to the next level of need.

2. SAFETY NEEDS, like physiological drives, are as much a part of the mature person's life as they are of the child's. Everyone requires structure and limitation. When people know what they can rely upon, what will happen next, where the ground is solid before them, they feel secure enough to venture forward. Psychologically, all human beings are able to function more confidently when assured of guidance and support. Emotionally and socially, few individuals can exist as continents unto themselves. Each person has a need to cling to the safety of the known. Men, women, and children who know in advance what to expect and what is expected of them enjoy a greater feeling of well-being. Forewarning not only permits forearming; it provides a structure and direction within which the human being feels it is safe to acknowledge and carry out his desires or decisions.

Paul was such a quiet, polite, obedient nine-year-old that the neighbors always remarked to his parents: "If only all kids were as terrific as your Paul. Well mannered, not noisy or fresh like some of the others around here."

108

What the neighbors didn't understand was that, unbothersome as he was, Paul's behavior was not normal. He was a victim of an unmet safety need. The boy's introverted demeanor resulted from his living in a home in which his security, physical and psychological, was in jeopardy. His parents frequently quarreled and physically assaulted one another. In self-defense, Paul had learned to keep his mouth shut and his eyes and ears open in an effort to anticipate the outbursts of his parents and protect himself. So strong was his fear and his insecurity that he could concentrate on little else.

Little else matters to the child who does not feel safe. Troubled or threatened by real and imagined dangers, he becomes totally consumed in his search for protection, for consistency, for safety. Parental outbursts of anger, threats of punishment, name calling, rough handling, or actual whippings create more panic in young children than seems warranted by the physical pain these acts cause. It is the child's fear of being rejected by his parents which terrifies him so. Without them, he has no support system, no security, no safety. Similarly, when the child, young or older, is confronted with new, strange or unmanageable situations his security and stability are threatened. Nothing is more threatening to a child's need for safety than to be given more power or privilege than he knows what to do with. Total freedom becomes total chaos when children must strive, without success, to manage more than they are capable of managing.

Fourteen-year-old George had tried many times to get his father to sit down and have a man-to-man talk with him about sex and drugs and alcohol. The boy knew that he himself could only talk a good game about these things. What he really needed was some in-depth discussion with an experienced

109

adult, someone whom he trusted to tell him the truth. Father's attitude made it very difficult for George to get what he needed. Everytime the boy broached the subject, Dad turned him off: "Now look, son, I'm sure you know as much about the birds, bees, and booze as I do. What with television and everything, kids today know a lot more than we parents knew when we were your age . . . so . . . you just handle yourself in whatever way you think is right, fella. I mean, your mom and I trust you to make your own decisions. You're a darn good boy, and we're sure you'll make the right ones."

The burden of being totally on their own to decide what things they will do and with whom, weighs very heavily on the young and inexperienced. Total freedom is more burden than blessing. Children are victimized by a too-much-too-soon environment which contains no structure, no routine, no organization. Few boys and girls possess the necessary maturity to palatably chew all that they might bite off. If they have no safe guidelines, they are unable to avoid the dead ends and smashups associated with traveling too far and too fast on unfamiliar, poorly marked roads. The path to helping children satisfy their need for safety lies in only one direction—the direction of reliable and measured parental guidance. Unfortunately, many mothers and fathers, other relatives, and teachers feel too insecure to "chance" talking things over with the child. Adults are frequently uncomfortable about both what to say and how to say it. Even those willing to risk taking the conversational plunge worry about being swamped with questions they won't be able to or won't want to answer. They fear that what the child may learn from them is that father (or mother) "doesn't know best." What many parents don't understand is that they do have most of the answers their child wants and needs, or they can help him get them. The experience adults gain in living and learning creates a much larger body of information and skills than most men and women credit themselves with having. George's father should have encouraged his son's questioning. He should have welcomed the chance to give the boy the man-to-man talk sought. The sharing process would have increased the amount of information each one had and strengthened the quality of trust in their relationship. Should questions or differences of opinion have arisen on the touchy topics of sex, alcohol, or drugs, referral to such authoritative sources as books and social service agencies could have settled the problem.

One of the worst problems a young person faces is to be left on his own to get all the answers for himself. Nothing disrupts a child's feeling of safety more than an unlimited, "anything goes" environment. Nor is anything more confusing to boys and girls than the inconsistent parent who bars no behavioral holds one time . . . and imposes rigid restrictions the next.

Ten-year-old Terry was permitted to stay up well beyond his bedtime several nights to watch the *Johnny Carson Show*. His mother wanted company on those occasions because grandmother was still at church playing Bingo and Aunt Lil was sleeping out. A night or two later, Terry's mother put him to bed on time and went to visit a neighbor. Unable to sleep, the boy got up and turned on the TV set. When mother returned from her neighbors and found her son up late watching the TV, she shouted at him and pushed him into bed.

Inconsistent parental behavior, particularly the kind which is sudden, punitive, or without proper explanation, threatens the child's need for structure. Like a storm-swept ship uncertain of the direction which will offer a safe harbor, the boy or girl who can't depend on reliable adult guidance is likely to flounder. He is prevented from developing either trust in oth-

111

ers or the self-confidence needed to behave responsibly. Firm, fair and consistent discipline is the fabric out of which the best security blanket is made. This type protects children without unduly restricting them. It provides the psychological comfort that they need in order to reach out confidently and constructively for "love and belonging" fulfillment.

3. THE NEED FOR LOVE AND BELONGING is a basic social need. Human beings not only share physical and emotional drives, they have common social needs. People have a need to belong to someone or something . . . a family, a club, a cause, a crowd. They feel more confident and comfortable being a part of, rather than apart from.

> "I don't even care if they punish me," the ignored child reasons. "I'm going to get them to pay attention to me, no matter what."
> Desperate to gratify his need to be loved and to belong, he has little hesitancy in debasing himself by being bigmouthed or destructive. So intent is he to fortify himself with the feeling that somebody knows he's around, that someone is paying attention to him, that he willingly exposes himself to whippings and loss of privileges, just to be noticed.

Attention for a child is proof positive of affection; the younger or less fulfilled the child, the more closely he equates being loved and belonging with the amount of adult attention given. The time his mother or father spend talking to him, teaching him, or actively being with him, is the degree to which his sense of affection and affirmation is assured. If the child's experiences condition him to feel that the only time his parents notice him is when he does something serious enough to require their interference or punishment, the child misbehaves. The need to feel he exists is far stronger than his fear of punishment.

* * *

Gilda took whatever punishment her peer group meted out to her, and then some. No matter how many times they excluded her, or on how many occasions they ridiculed her, she always came back for more. Striving to belong, to be accepted by them, she did anything the other girls told her to do, even when they took outrageous advantage of her goodness. She was always available to do all the dirty work. She did it cheerfully and almost gratefully.

"I'd sure give anything to know the power those girlfriends of hers have over Gilda," her mother remarked to a friend. "Maybe then I could get her to be a cheerful Miss Goody-Goody around home, too."

Being cheerful Miss Goody-Goodys and dedicating themselves to excessive, and sometimes obnoxious, overhelpfulness is a common response made by ignored or unappreciated children. Other girls and boys deliberately damage property and relationships in their anger and frustration. Although the disruptive child and the self-depreciating youngster differ in their behavior, their goal is the same: Both want to be noticed, to be valued, and to be able to give love and get love as needed, belonging members of a group. The receipt of affection is as fundamental to the child's mental and spiritual health as food is to his physical well-being. Children who feel loved are more satisfied and secure. They know they matter. When a genuineness and abundance of love is given to boys and girls, they are protected against loneliness, alienation, and helplessness. Youngsters know there is always at least one caring, sharing person who will help them keep things from going wrong or show them what can be done when they do. The children whose need for love and belonging remains unsatisfied, experience difficulty loving others. Such boys and

113

girls do not like themselves. Not taught to know love, or how to exchange it, they pay a heavy price in loneliness and self-hate.

4. THE NEED FOR ESTEEM, like self-respect, is basic to human survival. We need the good esteem of others in order to develop self-esteem. Satisfaction of the self-esteem need creates feelings of self-confidence, strength, and adequacy. When this need is thwarted, unbearable feelings of inferiority, weakness, and helplessness result. The attitude of self-esteem is not an inherited characteristic. It is environmentally conditioned. Children are not born feeling capable or confident. The picture of self which develops is in large part a replica of the image reflected back from the eyes of others.

> "Boys and girls," the teacher announced to her class. "Please pay close attention to your new reading group assignments: Gloria, Ruth, Fay, Debbie, Paula, Evan, you are THE OWLS. Jerry, Cheryl, Bill, Steve, Pat, you're THE BLUEJAYS. The rest of you are . . . THE PARROTS.

It doesn't take long for even first graders to figure out the symbolic difference between a wise old owl and a dumb copycat parrot. The child who is labeled at school or at home does everything in his power to fit the description.

> "I don't know what's the matter with you Patsy; can't you ever do anything right?" Mother screeches. "Why aren't you a little more like your cousin? He's quiet, agreeable, and does things for himself, instead of expecting everybody else to bail him out of trouble like you do."

The child thought by others to be slow, clumsy, helpless, or hopeless sees himself the same way. The school boy or girl

114

unlucky enough to be picked on, ostracized, or otherwise devalued needs a specially strong dose of confidence administered at home in order to ward off the feeling of inferiority. Self-esteem is critical to emotional well-being. The mental health of a child is dangerously impaired when he is denied recognition as a worthwhile and capable person. When children feel good about themselves, they invariably feel good about other people. They want to please them by behaving appropriately; they seek to grow even more worthy of the esteem they feel for themselves. Satisfied, self-assured youngsters strive to build more self pride and earn continued praise from those nearest and dearest to them. Children who exist on an "esteem starvation diet" have neither the strength nor the spirit to become lovable and capable.

Most boys and girls act in accordance with the way other people see them—once again, the self-fulfilling prophecy. The child imitates the character traits he is led to believe he represents. Children told long enough and strongly enough that they are stupid, unworthy, or disobedient strive to live up to their image. Boys and girls told in the words and deeds of their parents and others important to them that they are decent, worthy, and able, gain the esteem needed to behave in decent, lovable, and capable ways. When dad takes the time to tell his teenager: "I really appreciate the way you pitched in and helped get things done around here when I suddenly had to go away on that business trip," the son feels appreciated and important. It is a good feeling, one he wants to keep experiencing. Even the small child is made to feel ten-feet-tall when mother, a grandparent, or the teacher commends her for her diligence, her honesty, or her generosity. The youngster knows she is "somebody" because she has been singled out as worthy by people older and wiser than she.

5. SELF-ACTUALIZATION is really the capacity to "make real" the person or the capabilities we know ourselves to possess. All human beings need to feel safe physically and emotionally as

well as to be accepted and appreciated socially. They yearn to know that they are valued as they are, for what they are. The need for self-actualization extends the individual to seek his fullest potential. A poet must write poetry, a sculptor must sculpt, a farmer must farm if he is to be genuinely happy. Many boys and girls never learn what they are capable of being. They neither know nor are given the opportunity to find out what will bring them contentment and success. The adults in their lives either place such severe limitations upon them or expect so much from them that youngsters are prevented from following the dictates of their own aptitudes and interests. In most cases, neither parent nor child can know in advance exactly what experiences or education are best suited to a boy's or girl's self-actualization process. Unfortunately, many adults are rigid in their belief that "they" know what is best for the child.

Carl knew that he didn't want to be in the college preparatory sections of high school French and advanced algebra. Since he had been in elementary school, he had wanted to work in a small nursery business growing and selling flowers and plants. The boy had two green thumbs. He loved the feel of the rich moist earth between his fingers and the thrill of seeing things grow. For six years he had worked summers, weekends, and after school in Huntley's Hot House, but now that he was a senior, dad had pulled the rug out from under him. He insisted the boy go on to the bigger and better things college would provide.

Everyone agreed that there were bigger and better things in store for fifteen-year-old Cindy. She was bright, beautiful, and beloved by her family. Mother and father showed their love by encouraging their daughter in every way they knew how.

They respected her past accomplishments and created a secure family environment in which she was not afraid to try new things or make mistakes. They listened to what she had to say and what she wanted to do with her life. They did not always agree with her, but they allowed her to make as many decisions as she seemed capable of making.

The girl who grows emotionally secure enough to separate herself from being a carbon copy of her parents has a head-start in becoming her own self. She can more easily become what she has the potential to become. Self-actualization in one area, or with one person, encourages a child to increase her effort to fulfill potential in other areas. Success breeds success. The boy who overcomes his shyness or "all thumbs" awkwardness is motivated to seek a leadership role with his peers. He may excel on the track team or get the best SAT scores for college. The girl who is actualizing herself vocationally is one step ahead in her ability to reach higher levels of achievement socially or avocationally.

Maslow postulated that the self or selves within a human being are in a continual process of actualizing, adjusting, and becoming.

Helping children know who they are and be the best that is within them is an important parental responsibility. Regularly praising children, honestly and openly, is the best way to encourage their self-actualizing. Praise is a far better motivator than blame. Blame results in a child feeling down and out. This depressed and resentful state causes children to wastefully expend energy in self-pity and anger rather than productively apply it to trying to do better. A wink of approval from Aunt Blanche, a verbal or physical pat on the back from grandfather, and the show of trust displayed when parents allow the youngster to make as many decisions for himself as he safely and capably can, motivate the child to continue doing what he is doing well. Adult encouragement and support cause a youngster to develop a good self-concept. He feels good about himself because people who are important to him and whose judgment he trusts have attested to his worth and capability. A good concept of self encourages a child to try harder to realize even higher potential. Conversely, youngsters constantly blamed or belittled lose or never gain self-confidence and self-respect. Too angry or frightened to accept the shortcomings by which they are labeled, many of them invariably project blame on others.

> "If it wasn't that that darn teacher just doesn't like me, I would have gotten a good grade on my English composition."

> "Honest, Pop; it wasn't my idea to start drinking. Some kid we didn't even know brought all this beer . . . and the other fellas started chug-a-luggin' . . . and they made me do it, too."

What both adults and children are made to do is largely controlled by their needs. The human need ladder is organized on a hierarchy from highest or most urgent to least demanding; the seeking, selecting, and satisfying that occur descend from the level of physiology to those of safety, love and belonging, esteem, and self-actualization. Fundamental to the development of a healthy, happy parent-child relationship is adult awareness, acceptance, and accommodation of the basic drives which motivate behavior. When parents react only to the surface actions or attitudes of a child without delving into their cause and effect, only shallow results are reaped. No genuine communication between grown-ups and those growing up can operate in such a vacuum. When John hits his younger sister for no apparent reason, when Mary lies about the use of drugs in her peer group, when grandfather reports that Bob took some money from his wallet, or when Peggy casually mentions that she's planning to move into her boyfriend's apartment—doing what comes naturally to parents may not be doing what is best. Parents need to ponder and plan before they pounce on the young. Whenever an offspring exhibits unacceptable behavior, it is not acceptable behavior on the part of mothers and fathers to begin exercising the tongue or rotating the hand before engaging the brain. No action or attitude exhibited by a child can be sensibly responded to unless it is sensitively considered. Responsible behavior on the part of mothers and fathers should be based on the following principles of human growth and development.

1. A child's behavior always has causes.

2. All human beings have the same needs, but children's behavior differs from adults' because their needs are expressed and satisfied differently.

3. The maturational level of the child affects his behavior. Being less fully developed than adults, physically, socially, emotionally and intellectually, youngsters often lack the experience to adjust in mature ways. They do not foresee the future consequences of their actions.

4. Whenever a child is unable to satisfy his needs, the resulting tension forces him to relieve the stress in whatever way he can.

5. Failure on the part of adults to accommodate the child's basic needs penalizes him unfairly. It makes the youngster feel guilty and insecure even when he is engaging in perfectly normal behavior. The boy or girl is deterred from successfully progressing to the next stage of need satisfaction.

Parents can avoid unnerving and unnecessary discipline problems with children when each bone of contention between them is treated in light of these principles, rather than in heat.

7.

KNOWING HOW TO USE "YES" AND "NO"

When old Mother Hubbard went to her cupboard to get her poor doggie a bone, she found the cupboard totally bare. The emptiness which faced this nursery-rhyme parent is very similar to that which confronts many mothers and fathers. Wherever they look, there appears to be little of substance. The external support systems which formerly provided physical, social, and emotional structure are in very short supply in society's larder. The discipline and direction once supplied by the extended family, the church, the schools, and the law, seem nowhere to be found. In their place are the less substantial values of the peer group and the media, which are shaped by the cult of me-ism. In the culture of the growing child, and in much of adult life, the concepts of self-denial and self-discipline have become social no-nos. Once, the one syllable word, NO, served to differentiate between right and wrong. Today, it is thought by many to be restrictive or unnecessary. Instant gratification is encouraged on almost every front. TRY IT, YOU'LL LIKE IT . . . DO YOUR OWN THING . . . YOU'RE NUM-

BER ONE . . . SAY Y-E-S. . . . Television, radio, books, records, and films entice! HAVE IT YOUR WAY . . . YOU DESERVE A BREAK TODAY . . . ENJOY, ENJOY. The cult of ME, MYSELF, AND I, the attitude of WHAT'S IN IT FOR ME?" and the selfish pursuit of self-satisfaction are dangerously appealing. Growing numbers of men, women, and children have responded to it. They have broken away from traditional values. Responsibility to others and personal pride in seeing a job through and well-done have become devalued. Converts to the YES generation say "yes" to whatever is easy—the easy life and the easy way out. They reply in the affirmative, not only for self-gratification, but to curry favor. Some "yes" men and women refrain from saying "no" to children in order to avoid confrontations. They prefer to hoard for themselves the time and energy that would be required to stand up and be counted as accountable parents. So persuasive and pervasive has the YES group-think become, that the forms of social structure necessary to teach children self-control have done a fast disappearing act.

Nature abhors a vacuum. Something must fill up the void left when the larger society outside the home falls apart at its structural seams. Of necessity, mothers and fathers need to assume greater responsibility for taking up the slack. The basic needs of children of all ages—for safety, esteem, and self-actualization—urgently require that parents, and all other adults who hold children near and dear, provide the structure, support, and substance derived from a *balanced* use of the words "yes" and "no."

Sixteen-year-old Judy came home from school with some "great news." The band in which several of her friends played had been hired to perform at a hotel up in the mountains toward the end of the month. "The best part," Judy explained excitedly to her mother, "is that they're getting free room and board . . . and Teddy's asked ME to go. Alice is probably going with Bill, the drummer, and we can skate and go sledding for absolutely nothing all weekend. Isn't that fantastic?"

After a long pause, Mother replied. "Well, I don't know, Judy. It's such a long distance, and who even knows if there will be snow up there then." Mother knew she was skating on thin ice.

Judy looked surprised, and a little angry. "Don't you TRUST ME?" she asked.

"What a silly question!" Mother murmured. She was fearful of opening her mouth wide enough to put her foot in. "There are still a lot of maybes to the whole thing, though, aren't there?" Mother continued. "Maybe Alice won't be able to go. And what about your schoolwork? Besides, you might find something exciting to do here that weekend. I think we have to talk it over with daddy, don't you? So let's just try to put the idea on ice for awhile," she joked. "Alright?"

It was no secret that neither mother nor father were very fond of Teddy. He was a bright, good-looking boy, but selfish, reckless . . . a little too big for his britches. It wasn't that they didn't trust Judy, but that they didn't trust Teddy.

As the week progressed, Mom and Dad both made casual references to the inadvisability of the journey. The hotel was a long, five-hour drive away; there would be too many people crowded into Ted's old van, jammed against the drums, the saxophone, and the electric guitars. Besides, there were a lot of loose strings on the question of sleeping arrangements, since all of the organizing had been done by phone. To all of her parent's comments, Judy nodded politely, then excitedly rambled on about how much fun the experience was going to be. Never once did she act as if not going were even a possibility. Why should she? Nobody had said "no," had they?

Knowing how and when to say "no" to children is a skill not well mastered by many adults. Even those who have developed the know-how find "no" difficult to verbalize in the face of the "yes" society all around them. Mothers and fathers of every age, occupation, race, religion, and region of the country, have a hard time finding the strength to resist giving in to youngsters. When the boys and girls insist upon doing something with which the adults do not agree, many mothers and fathers quickly surrender.

Among the parents who do find the courage and time to refuse, when that response is appropriate, there are some whose disciplinary action is too weak and apologetic. Not always confident about what to say or exactly how to say it, they hem and haw a little too much. They equivocate with, "Well . . . maybe," or, "Let's talk about that later," or "Go ask your father whether he thinks you should go." Whatever words are spoken to the youngster, he knows by the tone of the adult's voice, that "no" is not the final word on the subject.

When Judy's mother and father beat around the bush, rather than promptly stating their opposition to her proposed winter wonderland weekend, they were doing neither themselves nor their daughter a favor. They were forsaking their own better judgment, and their duty to her. Mom and Dad were backing away from their responsibility as parents to guide the sixteen-year-old. If "no" was what their common sense told them to say—what they really wanted to say—they should have said it clearly and confidently. No "ifs, ands, or buts" needed.

It is perfectly normal and necessary for differences of opinion to occur between parent and child. When they do, honest, open discussion between the generations should be the first order of the day. Judy's parents wisely took the time to hear her out, even though they took too much time to say "no" clearly. They listened with interest and respect when she explained about the proposed trip and her desire to go. Successful mothers and fathers follow this procedure of listening before legislating a decision. Wiser and fairer solutions to problems result when they are not made in haste, before both child and adult have a chance to express their views. Even when the verbal exchange has little chance of changing the final decision, there is value in a calm and courteous hearing of both sides of the issue. Reasoning together with a child helps grown-ups get a better perspective of his wants and needs. This information is very helpful in preventing or resolving future disagreements. The use of open discussion between parent and child rather than the imposition of adult prejudgments and dogma teach young people an important lesson. They learn to value the exchange of ideas as an appropriate and successful method of communication. Children get practice in listening, speaking, organizing their ideas, and making more logical decisions. By far the greatest advantage in letting a child have his say lies in the role model communicated to him. Children whose parents listen to them are children who more readily listen to their parents. The give-and-take between them not only makes for a more satisfying relationship, but it enables the boy or girl to better understand and more readily accept an ultimate parental ruling. Perhaps, after a more balanced and honest verbal give-and-take between Judy and her parents, the daughter would have seen the wisdom of their wishes. Perhaps not. Maybe she would have only grudgingly or grumblingly abided by their judgment. Possibly, she might have argued endlessly, accusing them of being unfair, old-fashioned, or evil-minded. It is even conceivable that the teenager might have defied their wishes and gone off on the trip without their blessing. No one knows for sure. Whenever parents must make an unpopular decision in guiding their offspring, they are rarely privileged to know in advance what their child's reaction will be. Nevertheless, adults should have confidence in their judgment. They should exhibit the courage of their convictions by saying what they mean without feeling guilty.

Like Judy's parents, most adults want to say what is on their minds, but they are fearful. Some are hesitant about interfering with the wishes or will of those growing up. They imagine that such control may frustrate a youngster's spiritedness. Even worse, it may antagonize the child into misbehaving more defiantly and destructively. Some men and women agonize about losing the child's love or companionship if they neglect to satisfy his or her desires. Whatever the reasoning, as a rule, many adults unwittingly join the "Yes Generation."

Fortunately for Judy, her parents were one of the exceptions to the rule. Despite their slow start in guiding her responsibly, they did say "no," before it was too late. Frustrated that their indirect comments about the inadvisability of the trip were not getting through to their daughter, mother and father shared their apprehensions privately with one another. With the courage born of togetherness, they agreed to have a talk with Judy a few days before the scheduled trip. They spoke to her calmly and openly.

> Look, honey, we really don't want you to go up north with Teddy and the band this weekend. We've sort of told you some of our reasons . . . the crowded van, the dangers of icy roads this time of year, and . . . there are other things we feel that are not so easy to put into words. It's not that we don't trust you . . . it's just that it's a strange place all you young people are going to up there . . . and when a group of kids get together . . . and they're really not under anybody's supervision . . . well . . . it just doesn't make for the best time, either for them or for worrywart par-

ents like us back here on the home front. We just
don't know how to say it any better, but we don't
want you to go.

Judy's reaction surprised her parents. The explosion they
anticipated never materialized. The teenager only looked at
both of them thoughtfully for a few moments, then she said,
quietly, "All right, if I can't go, I can't go. I'll call Teddy right
now, I guess, and tell him you won't let me go."

It was not until several months later that Judy confided to
her parents that she really hadn't wanted to make the trip
anyway. The fact that the other kids said they were going
forced her to ask for permission too. Judy had known that
Teddy and the crowd would have thought she was "chicken"
if she had said she didn't want to go. They would have considered her a "weirdo" if she had admitted that she didn't feel
such an adventure would be "super."

Peer pressure is a powerful and dangerous force on children
of all ages. The permissive, anything-goes "yes-ism" prevalent
in the preadolescent and teenage peer group is particularly
dangerous. Youngsters continually persuade other youngsters
to do things they should not or would not do if the pressure to
conform were not so intense. Whether it is going along with
the drinking, driving, studying, or stealing patterns of the
crowd, the individual young person finds it very difficult to
defy the group's code of action. The need to belong to the peer
group and to earn its esteem causes the kind of follow-the-
leader behavior which often leads to trouble. When Judy's
parents took the lead in making the decision which her own
confusion or lack of courage prevented her from making, they
were leading her in the right direction. By restricting the girl
from doing what she really didn't want to do, they were providing solid guidance. By showing her she could manage very
well without doing everything others did, they were encouraging her to more readily rely on her own intuition and good

judgment. They were making it possible for her to stand up to her peers, without running too much risk of having them look down on her.

There are many times in the lives of children when they desperately need a good excuse for not doing what all their friends are doing. Unable to stand up to peers on their own, boys and girls feel a welcome relief when they can complain to one another: "Sure, I want to go out 'cruising' with all you guys tonight, but my old man said I'm not stepping one foot out of this house if I know what's good for me" . . . or, "I don't have to tell you about my mother, do I? She means it when she says if I don't baby-sit with my pest of a brother, Friday night, they'll be a lot of nights I'll be going out without any allowance in my pocket."

Whether a young person requires parental restrictions as an excuse to get him out of doing what he actually prefers not to, or as a way to have a decision made which he can't wisely make on his own, the role of mother and father is the same—to help the child understand that the restraint imposed is in his best interest, both personally and as a member of his peer group.

Frequently, parents find it difficult to constructively come between children and their friends. Allegiance to the peer group and its values is very compelling. Even when a youngster knows in his heart that his parents are right and his friends wrong, he may take the side of the peers. Judy's parents successfully avoided this all too natural trap because of the manner in which they talked to their daughter. They did not attack or ridicule her request; they took it very seriously. They didn't verbally bully or belittle her or her friends. They did not pounce on her with a too fast or too furious "no"; instead, they provided a thoughtful and truthful "no." Mother and father communicated to their daughter that it was their feeling for her, not their authority over her, which motivated them. They confessed that they were worrywarts about the trip, not because they didn't trust her, but because they cared so much about her. They pointed out that the situation in which she wanted to involve herself did warrant concern on their part; it was a new and unsupervised experience very far away from home which involved many unknowns. Whenever young people are given honest, logical reasons for why they are restrained from doing what they want, they accept control more maturely. Even when parents cannot give a youngster the privilege he wants, they can give him what he needs—fair, firm, and friendly guidance.

"I WANT IT. I want it. That's what I want you to buy me," screamed five-year-old Ron, as he pointed to the box of Sweety Treaties cereal growing larger and larger before his eyes . . . until it filled the entire twenty-one inches of television screen.

"I want Sweety Treaties. I need it." Ron stamped his feet. "Jerry and Fred already sent in their three box tops and the money to get their finger printing sets, and if I don't," he began to cry, "if you don't buy it, I won't be able to play the FBI with them."

If any force, anywhere, is as powerful as the peer group in controlling the minds and the actions of children, it is the television set. Uncomplimentarily referred to as "the plug-in-drug," "the boob tube," and "Pandora's box," television wins the Emmy award for the greatest show of structurelessness on earth. The TV projects an undisciplined image of easy come, easy go; anything goes; "Yes-ism." Children of all ages are as susceptible to TV as they are to the common cold. The get-me-itis which television encourages spreads like wildfire. BUY ME! BUY ME! GIMME, GIMME! Nothing ever seems to be enough for the boy or girl. Adults find it difficult either to satisy or to ignore the barrage of youthful demands.

"I want you to take me to the store and get it," Ron urged as he moved from the picture on the television screen to pull on his mother's sweater sleeve. "I want Sweety Treaties," he insisted.

"We already have plenty of cereal in the house," Mother answered, matter-of-factly. "Besides, the dentist says that sugary sweet cereals aren't good for your teeth."

"I don't care what he says!" Ron's cries became louder and more persistent. "I want Sweety Treaties like Jerry's mother bought him . . . you're a mean Mommy if you don't buy me anything to eat."

"There are plenty of things to eat, if you're hungry," Mother replied patiently. "Would you like an apple or some raisins or a bowl of the cereal we already have?"

"No! I want that kind," Ron whined, pointing to the screen. "Sweety Treaties, Sweety Treaties. Please, please, please," he sobbed as his anger turned to exhaustion, and he hugged her around the middle.

Mother sensed she was caught in the middle of a no-win battle. Ron would continue to beg, sulk, sob, and make her feel guilty. Besides . . . she reasoned, emotionally exhausted, all he wanted was one or two boxes of a not too terribly harmful breakfast food. "Maybe, all things considered," she thought, "the lesser of the two evils would be to get him the cereal."

It is rarely the lesser of two evils for a parent to say "yes" when "no" is a more appropriate answer. Adult behavior of this kind encourages the boy or girl to manipulate parents. It teaches the youngster that might is right—the might of his tears and temper over the right of mother or father to guide him and teach him the correct way to behave. Whenever push comes to shove between parent and child, it is not only the child's wishes that should be understood and met. Adults, too, must to their own selves be true.

One strategy often helpful in avoiding the unpleasantness of the immovable object meeting the irresistible force is distraction. Carefully and calmly directing the child's attention away from the point of contention provides an opportunity for a more constructive exchange. When the contested issue is taken out of the spotlight, some of the heat is taken out of it. "Let me show you how to help me cut the vegetables for daddy's salad," or "Now would be a good time for us to play that card game I taught you," are ways to distract young children's attention and minimize the contention caused by a battle of wills. Strategies appropriate for distracting older children should take a form which respects their increased maturity and ability to redirect their own efforts. "Buck-passing" (Ask Dad!) or "spot promises" which the adult cannot or does not intend to keep ("As soon as I can scrape the money together, the bike is yours") should never be used. A safe way to circuit-break an overload demand from older boys and girls is to require that they provide more information about the possession or privilege they're requesting. "I don't have enough information to make a decision about whether or not you can take that job after school. Let's talk about the facts I need. You provide me with them, and then we can make a more intelligent decision together," Dad promises. "Perhaps you can go to the party, but first I need to know whether there will be adult supervision and whether there will be liquor or drugs," Mother emphasizes.

Should distraction be neither appropriate nor successful, the only strategy worth using is STANDING FIRM. Mothers and fathers should never allow themselves to be distracted from the reality that they are the parents, and that it is their duty to provide discipline for the child. Whether a youngster is an adolescent or a preschooler, whether he is requesting the use of the car or a box of cereal, parents should learn how to say "no" fairly, firmly, consistently, and without guilt.

Ten-year-old Charlene was consistently cruel to her younger brother Franky. She mumbled mean things to him and stuck out her tongue when she thought no grown-ups were looking. Whenever her father reminded her that she had failed to carry out some chore around the house, Charlene managed to blame Franky. Frequently, the little girl's hostility and jealousy toward her sibling was expressed in actions, rather than words. She hit Franky, pushed or pinched him . . . always accidentally, of course . . . or because, "He started it first."

Her dad was very uncomfortable with all the fussing, feuding, and fighting between his children, but he hesitated to take direct action, preferring just to separate them when trouble started. He continually appealed to Charlene to "be more careful," or "more patient," . . . because she was "the older one." Superficially, Father appeared calm, cool, and collected, but inside he was doing a slow burn.

One day his daughter stubbornly refused to allow her brother to look at her comic book. "It's mine and I don't want you to put your dirty hands on it," she dictated haughtily. This mistreatment of Franky was trivial compared to the many things his sister had done to him before, but the incident caused Dad to blow up. With all his accumulated anger, he suddenly lashed out at the unsuspecting little girl.

No matter how much parents try to shrug off or ignore their youngster's misbehavior, they cannot do this indefinitely. The irritation associated with each incident lodges within them, accumulating below the surface. Sooner or later adults find themselves unable to contain their anger. They let loose against their offspring with an authoritarian barrage of shouting or slapping inappropriate to the seriousness of the particular incident. Such a parental response is unfair and upsetting to the child. He or she does not actually understand either the crime or the punishment. Boys and girls are far better disciplined when parents deal with each separate misbehavior openly and promptly. The child then is forearmed against an excessively harsh attack because he or she is forewarned of the behavior that displeases adults.

Now, I'm warning you, Dick. If you insist on being so stubborn, I'll have to report this to your father."

"I don't care. I don't have to listen to you. My dad lets me do whatever I feel like doing," the fourteen-year-old boy challenged his stepmother.

Shrugging her shoulders helplessly, Dick's stepmother turned to the angry neighbor standing beside her. "I really am terribly sorry about what Dick did to your son but . . . as you can hear for yourself, there's no way for me to reason with him right now. I can't get him to apologize. Maybe it's just that boys will be boys, and your son and Dick will have to settle their differences between themselves.

The neighbor looked incensed, "You call what he did. . . . "

"Please don't misunderstand," the first woman interjected. "I don't mean to condone my stepson's actions. I really want to apologize to you for what he did to your boy. Taking a rope and tying him up inside your garage could have resulted in a very serious . . . I don't even want to think of the consequences. You can be sure Dick's father will have a word with him when he comes home from his business trip tomorrow night."

The night Father returned, he had to go directly

to the police station. Earlier that day a man had caught Dick letting all the air out of his car's tires. Outraged by the senseless prank, the car owner firmly held the strong, struggling, kicking, and cursing culprit until the police arrived. At the police station, the boy shouted that the man had beaten him. With the support of his permissive father, the boy's claim was officially registered. A complaint of technical assault and battery was filed against the innocent car owner. The charge stated that he had used excessive force on a minor.

As is sometimes the case, in this instance the law perpetrated an injustice. It confused the villain and the victim by fining the car owner fifty dollars. Hoping to draw community attention to this miscarriage of justice, and the coddling of the young people living in the town, the man chose to spend a night in jail rather than pay the fine. His decision to protest became even more firm when he overheard Dick's casual response to his father's question, "Why in heaven's name did you have to do a thing as stupid as deflating someone's tires?"

"I dunno," replied the boy. "It was something to do, and besides, I just felt like it."

Addiction to instant gratification—doing whatever one feels like doing, right or wrong—has taken a firm hold on American society. It has made the disciplining of children a more difficult task, and a far more critical one. Dick should not have been allowed to casually shrug off his misbehavior. A very prompt and serious father-son talk should have been the order of the day. The importance of respecting private property and the need for young and older to behave as assets to the society rather than liabilities, demanded discussion. The boy's father would have been wise to explore the real cause of his son's misbehavior. Was it a cry for help, or attention? Did the boy really have no better way to occupy himself?

Plans for better supervision of the teenager's time and for

Dad's spending more time with him should have been promptly formulated. After the two had come to some meeting of the minds, Dick should have been directed to replace the air in the tires or found some other way to right his wrong. Certainly, a sincere apology to the maligned car owner was in order, and an honest correcting of the police record.

When a child commits a destructive act against other people or their property, he should be expected to assume responsibility. He should be helped to understand WHY what he did was wrong and how to control himself in the future. In whatever way possible, youngsters who infringe on the rights of others should be expected to compensate for their actions.

Before it is too late, boys like Dick need to be taught that they may not let the air out of someone else's tires just because it's "something to do." If they are not told "no," and compelled to accept the limits set for them, there is danger of their disregard growing perhaps even to the extent of men who impulsively squeeze the air out of somebody's lungs . . . because they "just feel like it."

The sooner and the more regularly children are taught to be responsible for their actions, the better. From earliest childhood, boys and girls should be told "no," fairly, firmly, and consistently—whenever that response is appropriate. Parents can become better able to say what must be said when they recognize the three-way interaction that occurs between the permissive influence of society, their own actions, and their youngster's reaction to discipline.

1. The "Yes Group Think" is pervasive and persuasive in the child's peer group, school setting, and the larger society. Of necessity, the family must take more responsibility in teaching children self-control and self-discipline.

2. The conscious or unconscious habits of instant gratification practiced by parents themselves, affect

135

the way they guide their children. Some "yes" men and women avoid saying "no" to their offspring in order to save the time and energy required to be firm. Others want to avoid arguments. Some feel that restricting the child will frustrate his creativity or cause him to love his parents less.

3. Children need and want to be saved from the excesses of the "yes" society. They *need* parental help in standing up to peer pressure. Often, they are confronted with too many choices, easy access to alcohol, drugs, sexual promiscuity, and other forms of self-destruction. Young people may not readily admit it, but they want older and wiser heads to aid them in understanding which behaviors are acceptable and constructive, and which are not.

4. Adults who unwisely give in to the demands or unacceptable behavior of boys and girls harm both themselves and their children. A youngster's accumulated acts of disobedience, disrespect, or destruction eventually grow too large for a parent to handle. Sooner or later, the child gets mishandled by parental ferocity far out of proportion to the seriousness of the incident which became "the last straw." Unprepared for the onslaught, the child learns nothing from the experience, except that his mother or father is irrational and unfair. The momentary relief parents may gain through this release of pent-up anger rarely compensates for the feelings of frustration and guilt with which they are left.

5. Whenever push comes to shove in the "Yes, I will No, you won't" tug of war between parents and child, the use of distraction can prove to be an effective strategy. Young children's attention can be directed to a special book, a game, or a helping activity usually reserved for adults (such as cutting the bread under

supervision). With older boys and girls relief can sometimes be achieved by encouraging them to discuss the issues in a calmer moment, when both adult and child agree to apply less heat and more light to the subject.

6. Whether or not children are allowed to have the privilege or possession they seek, they should be respected enough to have "their side" heard and considered. They should also be given, whenever possible, the reason why "no" must be the ultimate response.

This kind of parental behavior provides the best means of helping children learn how to behave. It teaches boys and girls that "no" is an important limit setter and support system, not a limitless or illogical show of adult authority. Boys and girls are also helped to understand the distinction between the different kinds of restraints of "no's" parents need to use.

In succeeding chapters, four kinds of "no's" and the conditions appropriate for their use with children will be described. These are the challenge "no," the character-building "no," the convenience "no," and the lifesaving "no."

8.

THE LINE BETWEEN SAFEGUARDING AND SQUELCHING

One of Aesop's fables tells the story of a young shepherd who lost his life because he had not developed self-control. Tending his flock alone on the mountain slope and having no one with whom to talk, the lad became bored. He wanted his desire for companionship to be gratified instantly. The boy realized that if the people from the village below thought he and the flock were in danger, they would rush up the slope to help. So the shepherd cried, "Wolf! Wolf!" As the boy expected, the villagers swarmed up the slope in answer to his cries. Once there, they did not find the attacking beast they expected. They found only twenty sheep grazing peacefully, and a smiling shepherd boy who greeted them. The boy was very pleased that so many people had come to visit; he thoroughly enjoyed the excitement he had created. Several days later, again lonely and dissatisfied, the young man cried, "Wolf! Wolf!" Again, the townspeople hurried to his rescue. Again, they found no wolf. They had been fooled a second time. The following day even louder cries of "Wolf! Save us!" echoed from the mountain. Twice duped, the men and women refused to pay attention. Even when the shepherd's pleas became louder and more pitiful, they were ignored. The villagers did not know that this time a wolf was actually attacking. Uninterrupted, the wild beast killed both the shepherd and his sheep.

In fact, more than in fable, children's lives are lost by misinformation. Some boys and girls are too immature to realize the consequences of their unsafe actions. Others are old enough to know better, but they are too negligent or cocky to care. Small children are simply not alert to the many harmful possibilities which attend swallowing unknown substances or touching sharp, explosive, or electrical objects. Nor do they foresee the danger in wandering into the street or off with strangers. Similarly, preadolescents and teenagers miscalculate the risks inherent in hitchhiking, smoking, doing drugs, and sexual experimentation. The speed at which they drive and the rate at which they drink are examples of the daredevil behavior common to many young people. The excitement associated with risk taking, coupled with the mistaken concept of their own personal immortality, put large numbers of children in the category of an endangered species.

The saving of a child's life cannot be left to chance. Every precaution must be taken to keep children safe from their own immaturity and inexperience: What boys and girls don't know *can hurt them.* Responsible parenting requires that parents know when to say "NO," and how to say it to children. The physical and emotional well-being of young people depends on their receiving enough instruction, soon enough, about real dangers at home, in school, and in the world at large. Forewarning youngsters, however, does not automatically forearm them. Admonitions and explanations must be clearly, calmly, and caringly given in order for boys and girls to develop confidence in the giver.

To be protected against harm, children have to develop automatic obedience to adult directions. Little fingers on their way to poking a fork into the toaster, larger fingers curling around a knife, or unsteady teenage hands gripping a steering wheel must be redirected—before it's too late.

Even the child who has learned to obey and trust the lifesaving "no's" administered by adults is not fully safeguarded. Every boy and girl needs to develop self-discipline. Day after day children of all ages are confronted with temptations and choices they must handle themselves. Learning when and how to apply controls on their own behavior is vital to their self-defense. Boys and girls must be able to say "no" to the invitations of strangers; "no" to playing hooky from school; "no" to playing around with drugs, alcohol, and sexual promiscuity. Mothers and fathers cannot always be in the right place at the right time to keep their child safe and sound. Even if parents could, they should not be singularly depended upon to do all the suggesting, insisting, restraining, and reinforcing necessary to safeguard children. Boys and girls have to learn how to think for themselves. The ability to make wise decisions, independently, is the only thing which protects them from falling into the dangerous habit of blindly following anyone older or stronger than themselves.

Whether children follow the advice of trusted adults or use their own intelligence and conscience as their guide, they should come to understand that the lifesaving "no" is a friend, not a foe. Its purpose is to protect them, not to punish or frighten them.

It was terrifying! On every channel, the six o'clock news meticulously covered each gory detail of the slaying. BODY OF EIGHT-YEAR-OLD BOY FOUND BRUTALLY BEATEN IN WOODS BEHIND CITY PLAY-GROUND. Blood splattered socks and shoes found tied to the wheels of bicycle. CORONER'S EXAMINA-TION REVEALS EVIDENCE OF REPEATED SEXUAL AT-TACKS. With a flourish, Andy's mother rushed to turn off the TV set. She was determined to divert her eight-year-old son's mind from the pictures to which his eyes had been attentively glued. "Who wants to hear all those terrible sick things . . . I don't! I don't think they should be allowed to show that on television," Mrs. Anderson chattered nervously. "Finish your string beans, honey, and let's all think happy thoughts—like about the apple pie we're having for dessert."

Quietly, but deliberately, grandmother rose from the table and flicked the set back on. "Seems to me it's more important for the child to think about this than about apple pie," she said.

"Are you crazy?" Mother shot back. "You're telling me it's right for him to watch all that trash? . . . You're going to scare the living daylights out of Andy. He's going to be afraid to move out of this house, if I leave it to you—afraid to talk to anybody, afraid . . . is that how you want your grandson to grow up? Running into your bed every night because his head is full of bad dreams from all this?" Mother's voice rose hysterically.

"Now, just you calm yourself down a bit," Granny urged. "If you ask me, daughter, you're the one upsetting the boy, not the television!"

Andy's mother's heavy breathing eased a little, but her eyes still held fire.

"Bertha," the grandmother continued softly, looking into her daughter's frightened eyes, "You and I know there's a world out there that's rough and ugly . . . and the boy's got to learn about it . . . it's best *you* tell him before he has to get it put on him the hard way. Even if ya' got to scare him a little . . . well," Granny sighed, "it's worth it. The important thing is readying the child for staying safe!"

Better safe than sorry! Better late than never! Best of all, better for eight-year-old Andy to learn about the dangers of playing in unfamiliar and deserted areas before he sees its consequences in living color! The child who receives early instruction in ways to safeguard himself from possible harm is given double protection. He is better prepared to avoid any number of possible incidents, such as being molested, poisoned, burned, or run over by a car. He is also shielded from the anxiety which results when boys and girls are overprotected or constantly nagged with warnings of impending disaster. Andy's mother's compulsion to save her son from being exposed to the violence depicted on the TV screen was natural. But it was also naive. Granny knew that forewarning children forearms them, but she was not totally correct either. In her effort to protect her grandson's life, she overlooked the risks of frightening him to death. Andy could not and should not have been protected from the facts of real life. Little as he was, he needed to be prepared to deal with them. What the boy should have been given from both of the people who loved him was a careful nonthreatening explanation of what the TV news was detailing. The youngster needed to be assured that the gruesome things he saw or the horrid things he might hear about do not happen every day, or to all children. Quite matter-of-factly, Andy should have been told that the people who loved him and wanted to make sure he kept safe had made some rules to help him keep out of danger. The family safety rules should then have been described or re-explained to the boy— that he was not to play in deserted or dark areas alone, not to talk to or go off with strangers, no matter what they promised, and not to leave the door unlocked when he was at home alone. Giving too many warnings at such a time would only have served to confuse and scare the boy. Two or three of the most important ones, explained carefully but unfrighteningly, would make Andy more knowledgeable and less anxious about the unknown.

143

Fear of the unknown is more terrifying to children than the stressful things they may be aware of. The child who senses that an adult is trying to hide something from him experiences more anxiety then the boy or girl who has had a danger openly explained to him. The parent who clearly and calmly shares with children the risks of walking on ice-covered bodies of water, playing with razors, chemicals, matches, etc., generates less anxiety in them than the mother or father who tries to "cover up" the truth. Ignorance is not bliss. Children who "see no evil, hear no evil, speak no evil" are not shielded from it. They are more likely to get involved in trouble. Conversely, boys and girls exposed too suddenly to new and frightening situations run a greater risk of being traumatized by the experience rather than educated by it. When the dire consequences of playing in isolated areas, touching electrical appliances, or fighting with a sibling are exaggerated or detailed too threateningly, a boy or girl may become abnormally anxious about them. The child may not want to participate in new experiences which are normal and safe. Warning a child too suddenly or too alarmingly about the consequences of opening the door to a stranger can result in his becoming terrified every time the doorbell rings. The youngster made abnormally fearful of vile people lurking outside her home, on the buses, in the playground, around the grocery store, can become so overanxious that she feels uncomfortable talking to anyone she doesn't know. Even when that child grows older, she may not outgrow her terror of exposure to the risks of new experiences and new people. She may shy away from participating in unfamiliar situations. Fear of doing something wrong, or something risky, prevents people of all ages from doing anything at all.

Careful parental planning is an important first step in protecting children without petrifying them. Adults should introduce boys and girls to the facts of life before the fact, not after. At every age, youngsters should learn what they may safely do, what is unsafe, and why. Boys and girls need to feel free to ask questions and talk about their fears. They should be encouraged to share with parents their own ideas for keeping safe and sound. The kinds of things their friends talk about should also be openly discussed. A "safety first" dialogue between grown-ups and those growing up serves two purposes. The child gains the safe feeling which comes from realizing Mom and Dad know and understand how he feels, and parents are able to determine whether the youngster knows and understands enough about keeping safe for his own good.

Even before he heard the splashing sounds and the muffled scream, Mr. Weber felt uneasy. His six-year-old son Jed had been too quiet. He had gone in to take his nap too willingly, particularly since the oppressive heat of the summer sun made his small bedroom feel like an oven. Making sure his son was safely resting, Father had taken the opportunity to go up to the attic to search for some old bank deposit slips and bills.

As soon as he heard the noises outside, Bob Weber rushed down the stairs and shot out of the house toward the swimming pool. A chill swept over him, although the temperature hovered at 96 degrees. Surely that couldn't be Jed's shadow in the far end of the water; he was in his room asleep, wasn't he? With a diving leap, the father entered the deep end of the pool and pulled his gasping six-year-old to the surface. At poolside, he pumped rhythmically against the little boy's chest. The motion caused his son to spit up large gulps of water which had clogged his throat and nose, making breathing difficult. Dad held the boy against his chest lovingly; "It's OK fella, you're all right now," he soothed. "But you just cry it out if you want to, it will make you feel better."

Later, when the boy was calmer, Bob Weber understood what had happened.

"It was too hot to sleep," Jed explained, "so I called you but you didn't answer. I went out to get cooler, just like Mommy lets me cool off when I'm too hot. I went swimming . . . but all of a sudden the water was over my head. I kept trying to get up, but the water kept coming over my head more and more and . . ." Jed started to cry again. As Father held him close, his thoughts returned to the time, a year ago, when the Weber family was first considering buying this house. The children were thrilled that it had a swimming pool. Father was not so pleased as he thought of the droves of neighbors who might expect to be invited over on sweltering days. He liked his privacy on weekends and wouldn't always want to contend with a backyard pool party. Mother was concerned about the height of the fence around the pool. Although it did conform with city ordinance requirements, she doubted if it was really high enough to guarantee that no neighborhood child would climb it and risk falling in. Mr. Weber recalled being worried that Jed, their youngest child, didn't know how to swim, though his two older siblings did. Jed loved the water and seemed fearless in it. "That fearlessness, combined with his unpreparedness, almost cost our son his life," Father shuddered. What had gone wrong? The boy had been carefully warned that the water in the far end of the pool was over his head. Both of his parents had forbidden him to venture into it, even when he had his water wings on. They had methodically explained to him that he was only four feet tall, but the water under the diving board was twelve feet deep. That was two times as tall as Daddy, so even he couldn't stand up in it.

* * *

The depth of understanding which children possess is often misjudged by adults. Jed's parents took for granted the fact that he understood adult logic. They neglected to tell their son simply and sensibly, "You may *never* go near the pool or in any part of the pool, unless a grown-up is with you." Instead, they gave their son a logical explanation concerning the danger of deep water to a nonswimmer. The parents' intentions were good, but their intellectualized cause-and-effect reasoning was as far over their son's head as the water at the deep end of the pool.

Children from preschoolers to teenagers are frequently thought to possess more intellectual depth than they do. They are assumed to have a greater understanding of parents' expectations than they actually do. What boys and girls regard as safe to do or not do is often far more naive than most parents think. Children are smart enough to look directly at an adult when he or she is talking. This attentiveness creates the illusion that the child is listening and learning. Nothing could be farther from the truth. Many times, boys and girls look, but they do not hear. When youngsters speak, many simply mouth adult words and talk a good game. Penetrating adult observation reveals that these youngsters' mature words belie the immaturity of their actions. However big or small a child is, he should not, like a book, be judged by his "cover." The younger the child, the more necessary it is for adults to take nothing for granted.

A good way of making certain the child understands and can be relied upon to obey the life saving "no's" is to set up a testing situation. Either a simulated experience or a real one can serve as a protective strategy to check the extent of the child's memory and maturity. "What would you do if you were very hot and wanted to cool off in the swimming pool or the lake, but no adult was nearby to give you permission? What is the first thing you need to do if you smell smoke, or your sister falls down and hurts her head?" The response given by a child to these hypothetical situations is a good indication of whether or not he thoroughly understands what safety requires. Frequent discussions with boys and girls of all ages which require them to verbalize their decision-making powers are the best preventive strategy for keeping them safe. "What would you do" the adolescent is asked, "if the kids who were supposed to drive you home from the party had a little too much to drink?" "How hard would it be," the preadolescent is asked, "for you to say NO to a friend who dared you to do something you had been told not to do, or which you knew was dangerous?" Occasionally, the child's precautionary sense can be tested in an actual rather than in a simulated situation. This procedure is particularly useful with preschoolers and boys and girls below eight years of age. The logic of cause and effect is not well understood by younger children. They have not matured enough conceptually to realize the relationship between shooting the pellet from a toy gun down their throat and the likelihood of choking to death. If done in moderation, no harm is done in creating a testing incident for them, or in taking full advantage of the ones which naturally happen. A child who is not permitted to go swimming without adult supervision may be urged by a child who is allowed to, "to come on in and cool off." A youngster warned against getting into a stranger's car is offered a ride home from school on a rainy day by an adult unknown to him, but known to the family. A youngster forbidden to touch any bottles in the liquor cabinet finds the door is left wide open one day when no one is home. Each situation forces the youngster to make an independent decision. One child might readily act on his natural or naive inclination to have fun, without considering the cautions or the consequences. Another might act on his recollection of the rules and on his resolve to follow them. Depending upon what choice the child makes, the adults guiding him are afforded the opportunity to either praise him for his obedience, correct his misunderstanding, or reprimand him for his disobedience. Praise is a very strong motivator for boys and girls. Any time the child's adherence to the life saving "no" can be praised, it should be. In this way, two goals are accomplished: The youngster's resolve to continue the kind of behavior which results in his being esteemed is reinforced; and, he is also encouraged to think before acting in other decision-making situations. Though this forearming device can be especially valuable with young children, its use should be restricted and discriminating.

Parents should be careful, though, not to overuse the testing strategy. A boy or girl rightfully resents being spied upon or trapped, even when the adult's motivation is in the child's best interest. Children become suspicious and alienated when parents constantly question their intelligence or obedience. Though this forearming device can be especially valuable with young children, its use should be restricted and discriminating. If wisely used, parents can check on two important issues: Their ability to communicate what they mean, and the child's ability to apply self-discipline whenever, and in whatever way, it is expected.

Elizabeth was expecting a baby. She was a fourteen-old-old child . . . carrying another child inside of her. The teenage boyfriend, whom she had been going steady with since the sixth grade, admitted to being the proud father. Three years older than she, he was a high school dropout, pumping gas in a local garage. Kip was a loner; he was a boy who never seemed to get along with anyone, including his own parents. A "man-child" who had deep feelings of being unloved and unrespected, the teenager's reaction to his fatherhood was not unnatural. He wanted to marry Elizabeth. He wanted to accept responsibility for his act. This made him feel good. He saw it as living proof of his personal character and chivalry. The big man, "I'll take care of everything" image, instilled a feeling of pride and power in Kip. Unfortunately, it did not give him the power to think straight. He did not analyze his situation carefully, nor did he question whether his behavior and his bravado were a way of feeding his own inner need for self-worth.

On the surface, fatherhood represented flesh and blood verification of machismo—manhood. What the teenager was too inexperienced to realize was that fatherhood is also a social, emotional, and economic commitment that can be a torturous trap for young people not experienced enough or committed enough for the responsibility.

As far as Elizabeth was concerned, the chance to play house seemed romantic and reassuring. What could be cozier than a little love nest, complete with baby and a man? Prematurely triggered by maternal instincts difficult to handle, the teenager's sense of judgment had become obscured. "A BABY," she thought ecstatically—"someone to hold and dress up pretty. A BABY—someone all my own," Elizabeth romanticized, "someone to love who will always love me back."

When Elizabeth's guardian learned of the girl's pregnancy, her first reaction was to scream at the teenager, to shake her and shame her. Aunt Florence, the sister of the woman who had abandoned Elizabeth many years before, found it difficult to resist the urge to punish this wayward girl. Elizabeth had humiliated her and Uncle Joe. They had given her their loving home, their religious convictions, and themselves, two hardworking, upstanding role models. In return, she had brought them shame and trouble. She had repaid their love and trust by sneaking around and having sex with Kip!

"No, Kip will not step inside this house to talk

things over with Uncle Joe and me," Aunt Florence shrieked at a weeping Elizabeth.

"No, you are not going to leave school this semester, no matter how terrible you think you're going to look! You should have thought about how you'd look before you started . . . before you . . . fooled around. Now I don't want to hear one more word about Kip. No, No, No!"

Unfortunately, Aunt Florence's controls came too late to save Elizabeth. The physical and emotional harm had been done. No matter how many "no's" were said after the fact, the teenager could not walk away from her experience unscarred. With an abundance of adult understanding and guidance, however, she could still keep her life intact. Elizabeth's guardian would have to rise above her own anger, embarrassment, and vindictiveness. Both she and Uncle Joe needed to find room in their hearts to adopt a patient, supportive, nonjudgmental attitude toward their niece. What was done was done. They had to let Elizabeth know that it was her impulsive behavior, not herself, as a total human being, toward which their disapproval was directed.

Convincing her would not be easy. The youngster would be suspicious and defensive. Nothing would be gained if the adults' actions created even greater animosity in the fourteen-year-old. Elizabeth had to respect and trust her aunt and uncle, otherwise nothing they advised or did could work toward solving her problem. Aunt Florence and Uncle Joe had to deal with both the emotional state and the physical condition of their niece. This situation required that they preserve the girl's self-respect, while imposing appropriate restrictions on her immediate and future actions. Elizabeth had to understand that the "no's" which would now need to be applied were meant to protect, not punish her.

The most intelligent course of action was for everyone to sit down and reason together. Neither Kip, his parents, nor any other person concerned could be excluded. Each one needed to be afforded the opportunity to express his opinion and to ask questions and give answers. Whatever anybody proposed needed to be considered rather than condemned. When one person talked, it was essential for the others to listen, and listen carefully. The options available, such as abortion, adoption, keeping the baby without getting married, or getting married had to be thoughtfully and thoroughly discussed. The economic and social consequences associated with each choice required careful examination. Not only the short-term responsibilities of individual options, but their long-term prospects had to be honestly faced. The future of the baby, Kip, and Elizabeth had to be considered sensitively and sensibly. Moreover, Elizabeth's and Kip's understanding of self-control and its implications for the future had to be dealt with. Both had to learn from their experience rather than merely survive it. Their impulsiveness had to serve as a stepping stone to safer, more self-disciplined behavior—it could not be allowed to become a stumbling block to their feelings of self-worth or to their chance to make the most of their potential.

Saving youngsters after they have gotten into trouble is much more difficult than trying to prevent poor habits of self-control from turning into serious problems. Bad habits are not easily replaced by good ones. The unacceptable behavior must first be uncovered and other, more suitable behavior learned in its place. From the preschooler who develops a propensity for playing with matches or putting unknown substances into his mouth to the adolescent who recklessly guns his cycle above the speed limit, smokes two packs a day, devours a six-pack in one sitting, or pops pills—lack of self-control abounds. If no firm and consistent cease and desist mechanism is applied to curtail a bad habit, the habit becomes necessity.

Two of the most effective controls for keeping children safe, not sorry, are adequate information and good parental supervision. Well before reaching the age of puberty (certainly by ten in girls and eleven in boys), children should be exposed to clear and complete information about "everything they ever needed to know about sex but were afraid to ask." No boy or girl should learn the facts of life in the streets or on the sly. Under the sensible, sensitive guidance of adults at home and in school youngsters ought to be familiarized with their own sexuality. They should be fearlessly prepared for the onset of the normal and natural biological urges which churn inside of preadolescents and adolescents. Every boy and girl ought to develop an understanding of the reasons for self-control and the consequences resulting from lack of self-discipline. He and she should be taught that appropriately and safely gratifying or controlling physical desires is not easy, but it is necessary. The safest way to approach the facts of life with children is to encourage them to discuss their feelings and fears openly. Neither sex nor any other subject should ever be given the silent treatment. From the time the preschooler first shows curiosity about how babies are born, or sees something on television which involves human biology, he should be encouraged to understand sexuality. An early beginning makes it easier to develop a natural, gradual approach to sex education in which both child and adult feel less threatened.

Men and women should not merely wait until a child starts to ask questions. They must be prepared to take the lead in guiding youngsters through their childhood more safely. Parents who are at a loss for words in explaining the biological and emotional aspects of human interaction can find numerous library books and pamphlets to help them. These will say it all for them. The written material should not be palmed off on the kids to thumb through themselves. Sex education is handled best when it is in the joint hands of adult and child. Preferably, the person "nearest and dearest" to the child should provide him or her with the information needed. Should a mother, father, aunt, or grandparent feel uncomfortable or incapable of explaining the facts of life to a youngster, a parent surrogate can be found. The school nurse, a church member, a scouting leader, or a neighbor may become the substitute teacher. The job requires that he be able to prepare children without scaring them. Every adolescent needs to be properly prepared to deal with his sex drives. Whether it is his parent or a nonparent who is most willing and able to handle the "hot potato" of sex education, no aspect of human sexuality can be treated as too hot to handle. Children must know about a wide range of topics, including contraception, abortion, incest, and homosexuality. Care should be taken about when and how these are explained, but the rule of thumb is that, while a little bit of learning actually endangers children, a solid and thorough understanding leads to the kind of confidence and self-assurance most parents desire for their children.

No matter how much preparatory knowledge about sex a child is given, it, alone, is not enough. Structural restraints on children's actions are necessary to establish the boundaries within which they can safely gain experience. Neither steady dating at too young an age, nor late-night curfews should be permitted. When babes in the woods are allowed too much, too soon, they cannot help but lose their way. Twelve-, thirteen-and fourteen-year-olds allowed to steady date and spend their time alone with their closest companion instead of in the company of many friends run the risk of getting too intimately involved. Before they even know their way around, they are left on their own to "go all the way." Parents should discourage these early formal relationships. They should encourage children to mingle in larger and more supervised gatherings. This kind of socializing contributes to the growth of better, safer habits.

When a few of the boys in the high school band kidded Vinnie about his "sleeping around," they weren't alluding to his sexual behavior. The fifteen-year-old was hooked on drugs—uppers, downers, whatever he could get his hands on. Since he was

154

"stoned" more often than he was "straight" (alert, awake, or actively engaged in conversation), the other kids joked that he "slept around." He slept around the classroom, in the gym, on the school bus. His teachers, if they noticed, didn't seem to care or know what to do about him. Vincent was not disruptive, destructive, or disobedient. He was quiet. He didn't bother anybody. He just sat wherever he was supposed to be and snoozed or stared into space. At face value, he didn't look like a boy whose life was in danger. Beneath his half-closed eyelids, however, he was a victim approaching death at an early age.

Vinnie's parents were the kind of people who believed in leaving well enough alone. This included leaving their son alone as long as he didn't get in their way. "Never trouble trouble till it troubles you," his jovial father used to tell the neighbors.

"I'd hate to get those think lines across the forehead that all those professors and politicians have," his mother would admit to her friend. "My motto is—don't think too hard, it puts too much needless wear and tear on the brow and brain."

Neither Vinnie's mother nor his father exerted very much brain power on their son's behalf. He was a boy who was neither seen nor heard much. Though they indulged him in all the physical and economic necessities of life, they gave him no emotional sustenance. Vince got little attention, little affection, and little communication from his parents. Denied a human support system, he found a chemical substitute. Ill-informed about the dangers of using drugs, he slipped into the drug abuse habit at a young age. One way or another—physically, socially, emotionally, or academically—they would be the death of him. How would the obituary column read?

"Fifteen-year-old boy O.D.'s on neglect."

155

Many boys and girls die needlessly of neglect. They are victimized, like babies whose parents fail to have them innoculated against a disease for which there is a preventive vaccine. Children who could be immunized by the lifesaving "no" are frequently denied it. Some, who are given their "shot" or two, have a bad reaction. The fault lies in the way the substance is administered. Some children are given too large a dose. With others, an antitoxin is used long after they have already "contracted the disease" of irresponsibility or uncontrollability. Whether they are given too much too soon, or too little too late, children resent and resist the administering of any more innoculations. They have mistakenly learned to associate the lifesaving "no" with pain and hostility rather than with protection and love.

Child protection is one of the most vital tasks of parenthood. Use of the following guidelines in applying the life saving "no" can provide both an ounce of prevention and a pound of cure.

1. Forewarned is forearmed. The physical and emotional well-being of boys and girls depends upon their receiving enough instruction early enough to be aware of their own safety needs. Children are an endangered species unless they are clearly, calmly, and caringly given information about the many possible dangers to life and limb—at home, in school, within the peer group . . . everywhere.

2. Youngsters should be prepared without being scared. The use of scare tactics is dangerous in disciplining children. The child warned in a fearful manner against talking to strangers may never outgrow his conditioning. He may develop into a recluse, afraid of all new people and unfamiliar situations. Keeping children in the dark about the kinds of things happening around them (child molesting, suffocation in aban-

doned refrigerators, teenage pregnancy, etc.) is just as dangerous as overexposure to harm. The unknown is more terrifying to a child than the known. To some boys and girls it may also be more tempting.

3. Don't judge a book by its cover. Children are like books—until they are "opened up," it is difficult to read them correctly. Most children do stop, look, and listen to the lifesaving "no's" set by parents. This does not mean though, that their depth of understanding is sufficient. Nothing as serious as protecting a child's body and mind can be left to chance. Parents should regularly check, test, and analyze whether what they think they are communicating to the child has actually gotten through to him.

4. To thine own selves be true. Self-discipline is the best protection a child has against danger. His intelligence and his conscience are the only two guides he can always rely upon to be with him when the need for the lifesaving "no" arises. Parents who provide children with knowledge and structure give them the best role model for self-control. They help boys and girls avoid the danger of becoming their own worst enemies.

5. Habit, if not curtailed, becomes necessity. Children who engage in unsafe conduct become addicted to that way of behaving. It is more difficult to get a child to change a bad habit than it is to caringly nip it in the bud. Many times, however, the lifesaving "no" can be applied only after the fact. Special care needs to be taken to avoid the child's resentment, resistance, and defensiveness. A particularly patient, nonjudgmental strategy is required to help the boy or girl learn from his mistake rather than repeatedly suffer for it. Adults who serve as leaders rather than as

bosses use the lifesaving "no" wisely and well. Their purpose in "after the fact" situations, is to help fix mistakes and maintain their child's integrity, rather than to fix blame upon him or her.

9.

CHALLENGE, CHARACTER, AND CONFIDENCE

In the familiar children's story, *The Little Engine That Could,* none of the train passengers could blame the little locomotive if it failed. The bigger, older engine had not succeeded in pulling the five coaches loaded with evening commuters up the steep slope leading to the railroad station. After huffing, and puffing, the large locomotive let off all its steam—and gave up. That's when the Little Engine offered to try! As the small, scrappy substitute for the big engine was attached to the front end of the first coach, the Little Engine said determinedly, "I think I can, I think I can, I think I have a plan, and I can do most anything, if I only think I can."

Both adults and children admire the strength of purpose and self-discipline which characterized the little engine that could. How can the same self-reliant response to difficulty which the small locomotive made be nurtured in children? What course of action can spur boys and girls on to make a plan, and follow through, conscientiously and confidently? Intelligent use of the CHALLENGE NO and the CHAR-

ACTER-BUILDING NO can put boys and girls on the right track. They are motivated to get up and go in a positive direction. They do not give up or run away whenever they face a difficulty. Just as physical exercise contributes to body fitness, the challenge "no" and the character-building "no" shape social and emotional maturity.

The challenge "no" is best explained by comparing boys and girls to oysters. Oysters are both protected and trapped by their shells. Many of these small sea animals do little more in the course of their lifetime than float back and forth in their natural habitat. Some do achieve the best that is within them by creating a valuable pearl. Their accomplishment is the result of a natural or artificially stimulated irritant being imposed upon them. The discomforting condition mobilizes the animal to action. It secretes a lime liquid in self-defense, the substance of which crystalizes inside the shell and forms a pearl.

The challenge "no" acts as a similar kind of stimulus; it gives children incentive against remaining dormant or untested in facing obstacles. It also helps them produce the best that is within them.

Four-year-old Miriam was an unusually slow talker. Unlike other children her age who were jabbering away in six- and seven-word sentences, she was still pointing or using a few baby-talk syllables to communicate what she wanted. Medical examination failed to reveal anything organically wrong with the preschooler.

One day, Miriam's mother was obliged to employ a new baby-sitter. She carefully warned the teenager to pay close attention to the little girl's signals and grunts, because the child did not yet talk well. Five hours later, Mother returned home to find a miracle had occurred. Clearly and distinctly, she heard her daughter shouting, "I want milk. I want cookies. I want toy!"

"What did you do to her?" the incredulous mother inquired of the baby-sitter.

"Nothing much. I just told her, 'No, she couldn't have what she pointed to.' She had to try to say it. Then I told her to listen to me and repeat it. She needed to try a few times, and now I can't stop her."

". . . Know what?" the teenager added after a pause. "I think talking is fun for her. She's like, ya know, proud of herself because she can do it."

Personal satisfaction and pride of accomplishment are the important end products of the challenge "no." Children want to prove themselves capable. They should not be prevented from experiencing the joy of a job well-done. Overprotective and undemanding parents do children a disservice. Miriam's mother should have expected more from her daughter, rather than accepting the minimal efforts the child made. The reward to Miriam and her mother would have more than compensated for whatever frustration or struggle mother's calm but concentrated insistence that the child verbalize her wants would have imposed on Miriam. Learning is fun for a small child. The ability to talk and communicate in the same way big people do enlarges the child's sense of self. A child is encouraged by matching his developmental achievement in one area with the behavior of adults in other areas. Social and emotional maturity result when children are required to do what they possess the capacity to do, whether the doing involves speaking, listening, thinking, or some similar performance. When men and women do too much for children, or permit a boy or girl to do as little as possible, they hinder the child's growth. Not only do parents weigh themselves down with more than their fair share of responsibility, but they deprive children of exposure to both the necessity and the satisfaction of working things out for themselves. Children grow up immature, inept, and inexperienced when adults fail to exercise necessary restraints.

"You can't stop me! You're not my BOSS," Will shouted at his fifteen-year-old sister. "You can't MAKE me stay home . . . you jerk."

"Nooooo way are you going to the Cub Scout meeting tonight, kid. I don't care what you say or how you fight me," Sally answered.

"You jes get off my back . . . you . . . old witch . . ." cried her ten-year-old brother. "I'm gonna go . . . and YOU'RE not stoppin' me, ya hear? It's BADGE NIGHT, I told ya . . . and they're gonna give me my Animal Care Award . . . for the hamsters."

"Well . . . isn't that just ducky! They're giving YOU an award for the hamsters that would have starved to death if *I* hadn't fed them," Sally shot back, sarcastically.

"SHUT UP," Will replied, sticking out his tongue.

"Mother gave me explicit instructions about you. She said if you didn't finish doing your arithmetic papers by the time supper was over, you were not to step one foot out of this house. Now, I told you THAT when you came home from school," Sally lectured. "But did you listen? Of course not! You had to waste your time laying across your bed looking through all those stupid monster comic books."

"I'll do my arithmetic homework in school tomorrow, before class . . . I promise. . . ," Will answered more quietly. "It's not that much to do, anyway . . . and if I don't get it all done I can copy it from Arnold . . . OK? . . . but I gotta go to the Den meeting tonight, Sally . . . P-L-E-A-S-E?

"The only place you're GOING is to the telephone to call Mom at the restaurant," Sally answered, exasperatedly. "And don't think she's going to be so happy having you bother her at work," Will's sister added. "But until Mom says you can go out tonight, I have my orders . . . and they're for you to stay put right here in front of your arithmetic homework."

"OK . . . I'll call her! . . . then you'll see!"

Will's call to his mother did not get the "yes" answer he expected. Sally was always tough on him, but Mom usually gave in . . . especially when she was called at work and didn't have time to argue. This time, her "No" to the ten-year-old was firm. "You may not leave the house tonight until your homework is completed, and your sister checks that it's all right. Do you understand? . . ." Then, mother added, "You had fair warning, Will! You knew what you had to do before the Cub meeting. "Didn't Sally give you my message?" she asked patiently.

"Yeh," Will said softly.

"I'm really sorry you can't go to the meeting, but you have no one but yourself to blame, I'm afraid. . . . Yes, I do know how hard you worked feeding the hamsters and cleaning the cage . . . maybe you could call your friend, George, and get him to bring your badge home to you."

The calm, caring "no" Mother applied in dealing with her son was a challenge "no." In denying his request, she was neither patronizing nor punitive. Though she was busy, she did not give him the rush act. She took the time to listen. She

163

showed respect for Will's feelings by agreeing that he had good reason to be disappointed. She did not minimize the importance of her son's desire. Nor did she angrily or vindictively attack him for his choice of comic books over arithmetic books. The boy's mother simply pointed out the facts, clearly, concisely, and nonjudgmentally. Will had known what was expected of him, but he had not followed through.

Used appropriately, the challenge "no" motivates boys and girls to follow through. They are led to realize that the door shut against their going where they want or doing what they choose is not permanently locked. There is a way out. Youngsters are challenged to find it. The way may be through settling down promptly and getting the job done. Perhaps changing their approach, adjusting their priorities, or enlisting help from someone else will solve the problem. Through patience, ingenuity, or substitution of goals, they may be able to rise to the challenge. In using this "no," adults do not tell children what to do—they simply indicate that something else can be done. Children do not develop creativity or self-sufficiency by playing follow the leader to adult ideas. They learn by doing something with their own resources. Parents define the conditions of the "no," and children are encouraged to find their own solutions within the limits set.

Will's mother clearly spelled out the conditions restricting Will's choices. "You may not leave the house until your homework is completed, and Sally checks that it's all right." The rest was up to him. Left to his own resources, but with the feeling there was a way out, Will used his head. The Den meeting would be starting in less than forty-five minutes. Until he finished his work, he could not attend. Time was his challenge. There was no time to spend being angry with Mother or cursing Sally. If he started right away, without the TV on, and his sister helped him with the hard problems, maybe, he would only have to miss the Coke and cookie part of the meeting. He didn't care about missing that anyway.

Maybe, he could still get there for all, or even part of the Badge Awards.

The mind set prompted by the challenge "no" should set children's minds toward creative action. Only when their minds are set at ease is this likely to happen.

"You don't give a damn what happens to me," Kitty shouted helplessly, the tears streaming down her face. "I promised all those other kids I'd be there to lead the cheers. I have all the megaphones and pom poms and stuff . . . and tonight is the championship game. . . . I asked you a week ago if you'd give me a lift over to school with all the stuff . . . and you said OK."

"A week ago was a week ago; things change," her father said and turned the TV up louder. "You know how cold it is out there?" he added. "You'd have to get a derrick to pull me out of this warm chair to drive you to some stupid junior high school football game."

"It's the basketball game," Kitty corrected politely.

"What's the difference, football, basketball; all it is is a bunch of pimply-faced kids trying to act like men. . . . Besides, your school's not going to win."

"But, DADDY . . . you PROMISED," Kitty pleaded. "I've got all the stuff the cheerleaders need to. . . ."

"I'm going to promise you a good slap across the mouth, if you don't shut up so I can hear the rest of this program," her father answered.

"But . . . how can I get there? What can I DO . . . if you won't take me?" Kitty asked more quietly.

"That's YOUR problem . . . not mine! You

165

shouldn't have told those kids you'd lug their stuff over in the first place. Let them find some other slave."

"BUT . . ."

"I don't want to hear one more word . . . the answer's NO," father roared.

When children have no options, no one to whom they can turn, no place to go, they go wrong. They are not challenged by the "no," they are shackled by it. "No's" uttered by adults should NOT be so hasty or harsh that they immobilize the child. They are intended to activate the youngster's best resources. In the give-and-take between parental desire and children's preference, there should be no winner-take-all. Boys and girls reduced to unconditional surrender, or those ridiculed or reprimanded unfairly by the restraints put upon them, do not become independent and self-sufficient. They become defensive and defiant. The energy they could and should have used getting something accomplished is wasted getting even. Many times these youngsters get what they want no matter what they have to do to get it. The desperation and defiance which thirteen-year-old Kitty felt caused her to act irresponsibly. Without saying a word to anyone, she borrowed a neighbor's car, loaded the trunk with all the cheerleading gear, and tried to drive the fifteen blocks to Day Junior High. One half mile, two run-through stop signs, and a battered fender later, the car was up against the curb. Even before the policeman explained to Kitty that he would have to take her home, she knew it would be a long time before she had anything to cheer about.

When parents exercise the challenge "no" properly, children are not left feeling helpless and hopeless. Through tone of voice and choice of words the adult indicates that the "no" is firm, but not harshly inflexible. This lets the youngster know where he stands, and allows him to respond with his own effort. This increased involvement enables the youngster to use his ingenuity. Through the exercise of self-restraint or cooperation, he may eventually get what he wants, or at least part of it.

What Felicia wanted from her mother was not what she got. The nine-year-old fully expected the same service she regularly received whenever she forgot her lunch, misplaced her schoolbook, or needed a ride to the ice-skating rink or a friend's house. Mother would rise to the occasion and drop whatever she was doing. The pleasant, patient, seven-day-a-week chauffeur usually took her only child wherever she wanted to go. But this time . . . not so: the answer was "no."

"What do you mean you can't bring me the princess mask for my costume? I need it for the school play this afternoon. You know that!"

"I'm sorry, honey, but I just can't," mother replied. "I've had a terrible headache all morning . . . and I think I'm coming down with something."

"But I NEED it! I have to have the mask. If I don't, and everybody knows who I am before the ending of the play, it will ruin the whole thing," Felicia whined.

"What about Daddy? Couldn't you call him up and tell him to bring it to me? I don't really need it until about two hours."

"Your father is working at his office. He really doesn't have time to stop what he has to do to come home to get your mask and bring it to school," mother replied patiently.

"So what am I supposed to do?" Felicia demanded indignantly . . . her voice trailing off in a gasp of self-pity.

"I don't know," her mother replied, "but I'm sure you'll be able to think of something, honey, when you put your head to it. Remember how you were the one who figured out the best thing to do when I forgot my key and we were locked out of the house?"

The challenge "no" is a key for freeing untapped potential in girls and boys. It is a prod which helps children to help themselves. Felicia was not permitted to get what she wanted when she wanted it and eventually had to stop begging, yelling or sulking in order to think. The challenge "no" provided a forced time-out period. It safeguarded her against haste-making waste. The open-endedness of the restraint obligated the child to reflect and reevaluate, "Why did Mom say 'no'?" "What can I do about it?" By having to take a second look at what happened and why, the youngster was protected against her own impulsiveness. The very common "GIMME, GIMME" or "You do it for me" inclination of girls and boys was brought into line, allowing a better balance between dependency on adults and self-reliance to develop.

Being unable to rely upon "Mother to the rescue" did not bother Felicia for very long. She knew she could solve the problem herself. Mother had faith in her. This gave the little girl confidence. The best idea she was able to come up with took her to the art room during her lunch period. There, she spent twenty minutes with paper, paste, and paint, until something resembling a royal headpiece began to take shape. It was a little crooked; it didn't look nearly as good as the princess mask that came with the store-bought costume. But none of that mattered! Felicia felt very good about what she had made. More important, she felt very good about herself. She had done something without anybody helping her. She had succeeded in rising to the challenge. The youngster wished that the play were already over so that she could get home to tell Mommy and Daddy what she had done. Wouldn't they be proud of her!

Far more important than her parent's pride in their child was the sense of accomplishment the youngster felt in herself.

The sense of achievement Felicia felt was very strong. It was far stronger than the satisfaction she would have gotten had she persuaded her mother to bring her the mask. Not only was it stronger, but the self-reliance the little girl gained was of longer duration. The challenge "no" had given her a chance to self-actualize. She had become what she was capable of becoming—self-sufficient. Her small success in decision making and problem solving would give her a head start in meeting other challenges.

Children of all ages have much more inside their heads than adults give them credit for. Boys and girls are rarely required to use their fullest abilities. When the going gets tough, most young people have the capability to get going, but they are not properly challenged to test their mettle. Some parents do everything for children, making it unnecessary for the children to do anything themselves. Many who do nothing for children also do nothing to imbue them with the confidence or challenge they need to mobilize their own resources.

Early and regular exposure to small frustrations through the challenge "no" helps youngsters become more confident, capable, and self-sufficient.

Mr. Samuels let his son Jonathan win almost every Ping-Pong game the two played together. Dad figured it would be too hard on a six-year-old to get beaten all the time. He could become frustrated and angry. Repeated defeat might make the boy lose confidence in himself. Sometimes Father would shift the paddle to his left hand, when he thought Jon wasn't looking. This made it easier for the older man to throw the game. Jonathan never seemed to catch on. Despite all the practice Jon got—and the false praise—he never seemed to improve his game. Mr. Samuels didn't understand why! Since the youngster always won, no matter how he played, he had no reason to change. Not until cousin Gary visited the family during his vacation from school did things change. The hard playing ten-year-old didn't give Jon an inch in their Ping-Pong matches. The six-year-old lost every game . . . badly. Totally frustrated, he refused to play with his cousin any more. Jonathan insisted that he only wanted to play with Daddy.

Pampered children do not learn to try harder or do better. Men and women who throw the game to a child throw a monkey wrench in his social and emotional development. They make it unnecessary for him to tap his own resources . . . to plan, persevere, or prevail. Adults who let a child win an argument or a privilege just because they love him or want to avoid hurting him, love him neither wisely nor well. Anytime dishonesty or artificiality are used with children, they know it—even if they don't show it. In seeing through their parents, children see themselves as incapable. Mother's or father's excessive paternalism is proof positive that the child is not thought to be able to succeed on his own. For children to develop independence, self-discipline, and a good self-image, they cannot have everything done for them. Nor can everything be denied them. Both too-much-too-soon and too-little-too-late penalize children. A girl or boy who gets no chance to succeed is not motivated to try harder. He is immobilized. Too much energy is depleted by his tension, anger, and helplessness. None is left for working more industriously to improve.

However the challenge "no" is expressed, it should set limits.

Both Mr. Samuels' Ping-Pong game and cousin Gary's were off the mark. One infantalized the six-year-old by making success too easy! The other defeated him by making it too hard. The fairest and squarest way to interact with children is to be supportively honest. A straight line is not only the shortest distance across a Ping-Pong table, it is also the shortest distance between two points of view.

At the outset of any competition, physical or verbal, rules

should be established. A handicap system could have been set up for Jon so not only the best man won. If Mr. Samuels or Gary proved to be ten or fifteen points better than Jon, that point difference could have been accommodated. The game could have begun twelve to one in the boy's favor, giving him enough of an advantage to stimulate him to try, but not enough to assure his victory. Playing opposite to normal-handedness, or being obliged to place the ball in a more limited area of the six-year-old's side of the table, would have been additional ways to make the contest more even. (Were the game bowling, the child could have been permitted to bowl three balls to the adult's two; in Scrabble, or other word games, the child's letter count could automatically have been doubled; in horseshoes, he could have been allowed to stand closer to the stake.) Where there is a will there is a way to even the odds honestly. The thrill of competition is not jeopardized by such equalizing practices; the game is open and above board, with each participant trying to do his best. More important, the child is encouraged to give his best against the player with whom he should always compete—himself.

Self-competition is markedly increased in children motivated by the challenge "no." Girls and boys are able to succeed at their own pace and in their own way. They also develop realistic and obtainable levels of expectation. When children get into the habit of trying to better their own performance rather than somebody else's, they are able to avoid the frustration of unreachable standards. Their ability and their effort are brought into balance. The sense of accomplishment they obtain from their own improvement and problem-solving experience makes them try harder and become more skillful. Whether the youngster is prodded to improve his Ping-Pong game, or to figure out what to do around the house after Mom got rid of the TV, he must use his head. Whether he is being challenged to overcome a physical or educational handicap, or required to summon up the courage to accept the divorce between his parents, he learns a basic survival skill; he learns how to be on his own. He understands how to use his capabilities more effectively. The ability to compromise, persevere, make decisions, and be self-reliant is transferable in many situations. With the confidence born of a successful small experience, a child is better prepared to face new and more difficult challenges.

The challenge "no" and the character-building "no" are two sides of the same coin. They are more valuable in combination than separately. As the youngster succeeds in working out the conflicts which confront him, he develops certain character traits. Experience is not the best teacher for learning to be loyal, respectful, compassionate, and dedicated, unless it is orchestrated under the careful direction of adults. Being kind to a brother, tolerant of grandmother, respectful of someone else's property, or loyal to an old friend with whom none of your new friends want to associate is not doing what comes naturally to the morally immature. At birth, the child is an ego-centered human being. Physical growth and the accumulation of birthdays does not automatically insure that he matures into a more other-centered, humane being. His character is shaped not only by what his parents say and do, but by how regularly and actively they exert appropriate controls on his behavior.

"You know, Rose," her father sighed. "I just don't understand what's going on. It seems so out of character for you to snub Sarah like this."

"What's the big deal? I've made out my party list . . . and she's not invited."

"Maybe I just don't understand girls. . . . It's times like these that a woman's touch around the house would be a real blessing," Dad mused nostalgically.

"Look . . . about the party, I'm planning it for eight, OK?"

"You may not be having it at all," her father replied soberly.

"I just can't believe this is happening," twelve-year-old Rose exclaimed.

"My own father won't let me invite who I want to my own party. . . . Do I tell you what friends to ask over for your parties? . . . DO I? . . . Well, how can you say, 'No Sarah, no party' to me?"

"Because—Sarah is our next door neighbor," Dad replied.

"Oh . . . so that's it," Rose shot back sneeringly. "I have to invite her so you can face her parents."

"No, that's not the reason," Father's voice rose in irritation. "Now, I'm going to say this as clearly and nicely as I can. I wish I didn't have to explain it . . . I wish you, yourself, would have . . . well, never mind," his voice trailed off.

"Sarah was your best friend for over a year. . . ."

"Well, she isn't anymore," the teenager interrupted.

"She was your best friend when we moved into this house. You knew no one else in the neighborhood, and from the very first day, she came in and asked you if you wanted to play."

"Sure, big deal . . . her mother told her to," Rose replied.

"She didn't just come in once," Father continued. "She came in every day, walked to school with you, taught you how to hook rugs. You spent hours reading books together, talking together . . . you were great friends."

"WERE . . ." Rose emphasized.

"Then . . . something happened . . . about two months ago, I think. What happened? What did Sarah do to you that made you stop going with her?"

Rose's face reddened. "She didn't do anything."

"Well, why aren't you friends?"

"We're just not."

"Look . . . everything has a reason. If you can't tell me . . . at least be honest with yourself. WHAT HAPPENED?"

The daughter did not answer for a while. Her father waited patiently for some reply.

"The girls in the chorus don't like her."

"All right . . . the girls don't like her; I guess that's their privilege. What about you?"

"I told you she was all right . . . but . . . don't you understand . . ." The girl's voice rose shrilly. "It's her or them. If they see I'm palsy with Sarah . . . enough to ask her to my party . . . I know Sue and Babs and Erica won't come. And they'll probably stop being my friends, too."

Mr. Carter bit his lip. Instinctively he knew that he could not say the first words that came to his mind. Patiently, he explained to his daughter that he understood peer pressure, and that he sympathized with the position she was in. Then he said, "But, Rose . . . it's just not right. There's going to be no party in this house if the price that must be paid for acquiring new friends is disloyalty to an old one."

Of all the "no's" parents say to children, the character-building "no" can be the most painful. Unselfishness, compassion, respect, and honesty are not attributes which come easily to children. Ethical qualities can not be applied to cover blemishes in children as varnishes can to wood. Character is not a protective covering. It lies deep within and its fiber is the inner grain of the child. It permeates his being. The inculcation of anything as deep and far-reaching as a value system is rarely painless. The pain Mr. Carter's character-building "no" inflicted on Rose was a necessary evil. The importance of

174

teaching a child right from wrong requires such action. No girl or boy is born understanding justice, honor, or generosity. Even many older children have not learned to differentiate between worthy and unworthy conduct. They don't know why mother makes such a "big deal" when they swipe a little pack of gum from the grocery store. Boys and girls fail to realize why they are criticized for their inconsideration when they spread their books and athletic gear across two seats on the bus, while an older person is forced to stand. Some children can't understand why such a "fuss" is made when they tell a little white lie or "bad-mouth" the teacher. They simply have not been well-schooled in the difference between right and wrong. Nor have enough adults provided examples for them to follow! The standards of conduct have been fashioned, but parents frequently do not require that youngsters meet them, causing many boys and girls to fail to measure up in developing good character. Either they are unfamiliar with the yardstick, or fearless of its fair, firm, and consistent application to them.

"What are you doing to your brother?" Mother screamed at seven-year-old Lawrence.

"He hit me first!" the little boy yelled back, as he ran into his room to take cover.

Five-year-old Clarence was wiping his bloody knee where the truck, thrown by Lawrence, had hit him. The thumb on the smaller brother's left hand showed deep teeth marks.

Mrs. Whiting was beside herself. What was she going to do with Lawrence? Every day it was the same thing. He beat on his brother as if he were a drum. It wasn't as if she hadn't punished her older son to show him he could not behave that way! She had locked him in his room a few times, whipped him, and even bitten him once or twice, just to show him how much it hurt. Still, she had experienced no success in teaching her oldest child compassion or brotherly love. Would he ever grow up to act like a decent human being?

Growth in moral and spiritual values is the result of learned behavior. From birth through adolescence, character attributes such as compassion, loyalty, charity, honesty are built layer upon layer. As children grow, they can be helped to differentiate between socially acceptable conduct and objectionable behavior. Through the use of the character-building "no," parents teach children to sympathize and empathize with others. The imposition of behavior demands on boys and girls helps them acquire a set of solid standards. Demands alone, however, do not guarantee good character development. Youngsters imitate what parents do more than what parents say. Father can lecture long and loud on the importance of treating Granny with understanding, or the policeman with respect. Mother can sermonize and moralize night and day about being kind, truthful, or charitable. Most of the words adults utter to children go in one ear and out the other. How compassionate Dad himself is toward Granny, and how loyal Mother is to her friend make a much more lasting impression. Mirrored in the attitudes and activities of boys and girls is the image of the way their parents act. Children learn to behave toward others by observing how their mothers and fathers treat others and themselves.

When a child like Lawrence abuses another youngster physically or verbally, the most natural thing for a parent to do is what Mrs. Whiting did: punish the aggressor and comfort the victim. Many different approaches may be used to get the offending child to cease and desist: warning, whipping, confining him to his room, denying him future privileges. What the parent says, and the method used to discipline the child, determine how successful the effort will be in stopping the aggressive behavior. Moreover, the method chosen will have a major effect on the kind of character traits the child himself is likely to develop. It is normal for the adult to react with anger toward the child who is a bully. When he is bullying his own flesh and blood, it is likely that a parent will be even angrier. Frequently, without realizing it, mother or father respond by bullying the bully. They scream, hit, or treat him in a manner similar to the way he has treated his brother or sister. Rarely does a parental show of force of this kind show a child that force should not be used. The opposite is more often the case. Might is right because even mom and dad use it.

The best way to develop the values of compassion and understanding in a child is to be compassionate and understanding toward him. When he is not acting like his brother's keeper, the adult must keep from stooping to the child's level. Lawrence's mother should have tried this. She should have tried treating the offender as if he were the offended. Calmly and caringly, Mrs. Whiting might have asked her son what hurt him so much that he had to scream, bite, and throw things at his brother. Concentrating this kind of comforting attention on the culprit often gets to the source of the problem without having to get to the child's bottom. Holding him, listening to him, loving him lets a child see and feel the strength of forgiveness and loyalty he needs at the moment. It helps him understand that it is his behavior, not he, that is unacceptable. Most important, the youngster is provided a role model to copy in his relationship with others. Comforting both the aggressor and the victim strengthens the bond between them much more than words or whippings. Not as a punishment, but as a responsibility and an act of brotherly love, the offending child should be required to help ease the discomfort of the other. He can wipe the blood from his brother's knee, bandage his bite, and try in the best way he is able to repair the damage he has caused. After the physical needs of the attacked child are satisfied, both youngsters should be directed to sit down as friends and reason together. Greater trust between the two can be generated in such an atmosphere. They can be readied to share the responsibility of showing and telling each other how to be better friends.

* * *

"How come the phone hasn't rung all weekend? Are all your friends out of town?" Mother joked with Lola.

"I'm not sure I have any friends left!" the eleven-year-old replied, haltingly. "Ya see . . . well, even if Dad and you say it, I'm not so sure honesty is the best policy all the time."

"What do you mean?" her mother inquired.

"I wouldn't give the test answers to Bunny yesterday in school. I kept telling her to study, and I said I couldn't help her cheat, but she just laughed. She didn't believe I meant it. . . . Mom, you should have seen the sick look on her face when she tried to see what answers I had on my paper, and I covered it all up with my arm . . . I mean, she looked so scared and so mad . . . and . . . but, then she turned to Steve's side of the table, and I think he kinda likes her, and I saw her writing down his answers . . . Ya know, he's smart, so probably Bunny will get a better mark on the test than I do."

Mrs. McVickers took a deep sigh.

"Lola," she said, coming over to put her arms around her daughter and look her straight in the eye. "Today, I wouldn't even care if you got zero on the test. I'm more proud of you for what you did than I can possibly say. You did a very, very difficult thing today . . . something that even a lot of grown-ups I know wouldn't have the courage to do. You did what was right, even though you had to pay a very high price for your action . . . and I know when Daddy comes home, he's going to respect what you did as much as I do."

Lola smiled a little. "Yeah, I know it was right, but I'm still not too sure it was worth it. . . . Mom, I think all the other kids are mad at me, too. Do you think I'll ever get them to be my friends again?"

* * *

Whenever a child exercises good judgment or exhibits a worthy character trait, he should be commended. The praise should not be casual or cursory. The full depth of respect the youngster deserves for acting maturely and responsibly needs to be conveyed. Mrs. McVickers showed quick and enthusiastic pleasure for her daughter's actions. She acknowledged how difficult the task was that Lola accomplished. Mother's pride reinforced the little girl's pride in herself. Later, Daddy would add his kudos for a job well-done by his child.

The strength and sincerity of an adult's pride in a child's behavior spurs him on toward continued good character development. The good feeling a child gets from obeying the rules or doing the right thing is often not enough to sustain him. He needs the constant support of those he respects to acknowledge his ethical behavior and to commend him for it. Youngsters need to be rewarded for their good deeds—not in money or privileges—but with the best reward of all, the honest praise of their parents.

Although Wayne was as honest as a nine-year-old could be, his mother found it difficult to praise him. To tell the truth, the boy was too honest for his own good. He was so forthright that he hurt people's feeling. He was so frank, he was tactless. "Boy, is this thing dirty. You should really clean it out," he would say to a neighbor who gave him a ride in the car. "My mother said she didn't think the tomatoes you grew in your garden were half as good as the ones she grew," he expounded to Aunt Mary.

Wayne's habit of telling the truth, the whole truth and nothing but the truth, had gotten not only him, but his family in hot water. Mother wondered how she could keep things cool in the neighborhood and still encourage honesty in Wayne.

Any virtue carried to illogical lengths may become a vice.

179

Honesty, loyalty, generosity, or compassion need to be seen in proper perspective. Being too compassionate to a person can infantilize him and rob him of his independence. Rigid loyalty can fix a child in a cause or a group detrimental to him. When parents use the character-building "no" with children, they should both teach the kind of ethical behavior desired and how it is appropriately expressed. Wayne's mother had to be perfectly honest with her son. She had to tell him he needed to learn a few more rules about truthfulness: Unless directly asked for your opinion, don't say anything unless you can say something positive. When asked, remember, it's not what you say as much as the way you say it. Choose words that don't make other people angry or insult them. Speak to others as you would have them speak to you.

Spoken at the right time and for the right reason, both the character-building "no" and the challenge "no" help boys and girls to help themselves. The challenge "no" provides experience in decision making and self-sufficiency. The character-building "no" develops an ethical value system. The use of each prods children to discover their untapped potential. It motivates them to achieve a better balance between dependence on adults and self-reliance.

1. The challenge "no" stimulates creativity and self-sufficiency in children. The calm, caring, nonjudgmental way in which they are restrained motivates boys and girls to find other ways to accomplish their goals.

2. The sense of pride which results from the accomplishment of a difficult task is the reward of the challenge "no." Rarely are most children required to use their abilities and talents to their fullest extent. When appropriate demands are made on them, boys and girls learn to put their brightest and best effort forward.

3. Early and regular exposure to small frustrations helps prepare youngsters to handle larger ones. Confi-

dence and competence are the by-products of the correctly used challenge "no."

4. Self-competition is markedly increased when children are required to accept responsibility for their own problem solving.

5. Growth in moral and spiritual values is learned behavior. Generosity, respect, honesty, and compassion are not varnishes which can be applied to the surface. They must be imbued deep within the child if they are to be effective. For this reason, the inculcation of strength of character is painful.

6. Adults influence the character development of children in the following ways:
By setting fair, firm, and consistent standards
By requiring children to live up to these standards
By providing good adult role models
By rewarding children with praise and respect when they demonstrate strength of character.

7. The character-building "no" sculpts the ego-centered human being into a more other-centered, humane being.

10.

THE LINE BETWEEN HELPLESSNESS AND SELFISHNESS

Most parents know exactly how Gulliver felt after the shipwreck washed him up on the shores of Lilliput. Surrounded by the six-inch-tall inhabitants of the island, Gulliver's wallet, snuffbox, comb, and handkerchief were seized, and he was tied up and made a prisoner. Although Gulliver was more than ten times bigger than the Lilliput people who attacked him, he found himself powerless against them.

Boys and girls of every size impose the same feelings of powerlessness on adults. Men and women are regularly tied up in knots trying to satisfy the demands their children make. For better or worse, parenting is a twenty-four-hour-a-day, seven-day-a-week, three-hundred-and-sixty-five-day-a-year job. The responsibility mothers and fathers face in gratifying the physical, emotional, social, spiritual and intellectual needs of their offspring is awesome. Often, it is angering! With justification, parents feel overwhelmed by the time-consuming, dollar-demanding, energy-draining chore of caring for their children. The "Yes you will!" "No, I won't!" tug of war common in most households tries the adult's patience and good humor. By their nature children want what they want, when they want it, immediately, if not sooner. Most do not yet understand that there is a difference between what they'd like and what it is essential for them to have. Boys and girls are slow to realize that they don't need everything they want. Even fewer youngsters appreciate the fact that mothers and fathers have wants and needs of their own. As far as some children are concerned, parents are not people in their own right. They are Jackie's father, Glenn's mother, the allowance-giver, taxi driver, chief cook and bottle washer, and the disciplinarian. The CONVENIENCE NO upholds the natural rights of parents to exercise freedom of choice above and beyond their role as parents. It assures them the privilege of being their own person, maintaining their individual interests, using their time, and building their own lives apart from the togetherness they share with their children. Adults need to establish particular life-style patterns without guilt. By living a part of their lives apart from their children, parents teach them an important lesson in learning to live and let live. By learning to use the convenience "no" intelligently, adults build a richer life both for themselves and their offspring.

Nancy Evers needed all the support she could get. Her husband of fourteen years had deserted her for a younger woman. The court was trying to find him to enforce a nonsupport judgment. Mrs. Evers was forced to go out to work to support her two children. Each day, after clerking for eight hours in a large Five and Ten, she hurried home to fix dinner, settle the kids' quarrels, and supervise their homework. In between these chores, she made time to get Mary to the dentist whenever her braces needed checking and Brad to the saxophone teacher's studio. Longingly, she looked forward to Sunday, her day of rest, when she could read the newspaper, take a long bath, and just relax!

When thirteen-year-old Brad casually remarked that he was planning to ask some kids over for a Sunday afternoon jam session, Mrs. Evers was not all sweetness and light.

"No," she said. "I'm sorry, Brad. They can't come."

"But, Mom . . ." her son started to object.

"NO. It's my day for peace and quiet. I've had a long week, and I need rest badly."

"Well, who's going to bother you? We'll all be in the den. You can read or take your bath anyway."

"No!" his mother said more firmly. "It just isn't convenient for me to have your friends over this Sunday. Change the meeting place to somebody else's house."

"To whose?" Brad snorted.

"That's up to you," Mother said calmly.

"Boy, I should have known better than to believe all that stuff . . . 'Bring your friends home, Brad; your friends are always welcome in our house,'" he mimicked his mother's voice. "That was for the birds," he grumbled.

"Look, your friends have been here before, and they'll be here again . . . but not this Sunday!" Mrs. Evers said with finality.

"You ruin everything," her son growled, and sulked away to the telephone.

Failure to use the convenience "no" is more likely to ruin everything in the parent-child relationship than the use of it. Adults have rights, preferences, and ideas which deserve consideration and respect. Men and women are human beings, not sacrificial lambs. Those who foolishly offer themselves up to be used by their children let their own lives go up in smoke. They become shadow people by surrendering themselves to every whim or wish of the child. They lose substance as independent individuals. When excessive amounts of energy, anxiety, and time are showered on boys and girls, they are rarely appreciated. When youngsters are handed all they ask for on a silver platter, sooner or later the parent-child relationship tarnishes. The real value of mother's or father's all out effort to please, placate, or permit whatever the child wants is diminished. What youngsters get easily is as easily taken for granted by them.

The convenience "no" affirms the right of parents to be and become complete human beings. Boys and girls of all ages need to learn that mom and dad have feelings and frustrations just as they do. The child unfamiliar with this fact of life resents his parents' concern for self-gratification. His initial reaction to their behavior is one of agitation and hostility. "What's gotten into them that they're so mean? How come they never care about anybody except themselves?" When a parental restraint is used intelligently, rather than indiscriminately, the child's anger changes to acceptance. Eventually, the acceptance turns to respect. Children respect fairness, firmness, and consistency. They admire adults who respect themselves enough to say "no."

Brad's mother used the convenience "no" intelligently. She applied a reasonable time limit to her "no" (that particular Sunday); she gave him a logical reason for her denial (her personal need for quiet). By standing firm, Mrs. Evers was able to avoid stooping to Brad's level. She did not become defensive, fighting fire with fire when Brad back talked and challenged her honesty; she kept to the issue, firmly and pleasantly. The convenience "no" more than the lifesaving, challenge or character-building "no," elicits anger and indignation. Boys and girls are more capable of seeing that other restraints are for their own benefit. They find it difficult to see the convenience "no" as more than an oppressive, arbitrary decision, catering only to a selfish whim on the part of parents. "Well, who's going to bother you . . . you can read or take your bath anyway," Brad chided his mother. Like numerous other young people, he was oblivious to the fact that his mother had a legitimate right to have a decision fit her needs, rather than her needs fit a potential situation.

Boys and girls of all ages should be helped to understand that it is neither unnatural nor undesirable for adults to consider their own convenience and concerns. It is selfish for boys and girls to expect them to do otherwise.

"Hey, Mom; you're expected to be at school promptly at eight o'clock Monday morning, otherwise you'll have to get a late slip from the office, I guess." Diane laughed. She dropped her books on the hall table and walked toward the kitchen.

"In school early Monday morning? For what?" the ten-year-old's mother inquired.

"Yep, I had to volunteer you today for the class trip to the Science Museum," Diane answered, stuffing a donut into her mouth.

"You what?" Mrs. Bronston exclaimed.

"Like they taught us about the slaves in that history book you read with me, Mom, I indentured you or something," the little girl answered, reaching for another donut. "That means I sold you, doesn't it? Anyway, you're gonna be one of the monitor mothers for our bus trip, Monday, OK?"

"No, I'm afraid it's not OK," Mother replied determinedly.

"Oh, don't tell me you already have something else you're supposed to do," her daughter pleaded excitedly. "Mom, you'll have to change it because. . . ."

"I don't have any other place to go," Mrs. Bronston replied. "But I'm staying right here at home,

Monday, because I need time for myself. Monday is the only morning I don't do volunteer work at the hospital."

"I knew that," Diane said. "That's why I told them you could go on the trip."

"But I'm not going. You'll have to uninvite me . . . or is it unindenture," Mother tried to joke.

"But, Mom, I already told our teacher, Mr. Harris, and he expects you. Besides . . . the class may not be able to go at all if we're short an adult helper. The school has this safety rule or something about it."

"You'd better call Mr. Harris then, while he's probably still at school, and tell him to get someone else."

"But why . . . why can't you?" Diane whined.

"Because it's just not convenient for me to go, that's why. Next time, before you make any plans for me, check to see if I agree. That way you'll avoid making promises you can't keep . . . and you'll also be acting a lot more courteously to me."

It is not only courteous, but crucial that adults know what to expect before pressure is put on them by children. Mothers and fathers require structure in their lives in the same way that children do. Everyone operates less anxiously and more effectively when he or she knows what's coming. Preparation prevents desperation. Sudden expectations are like sudden noises and sudden changes; they are unnerving. Parents who are not given enough advance notice to accommodate their own interest and time preferences get uptight when they allow themselves to be at the beck and call of children. Men and women lose self-control. Adults who serve as puppets in the hands of boys and girls never know which way the strings will be pulled next. They put themselves in danger of being pulled too far away from their own interests.

Diane's mother was strong enough to be fair to herself. She refused to be caught in the trap her ten-year-old had set. Well-baited as it was, with the promise already made to the teacher, and the possibility that the whole trip hung in the balance if she refused, Mrs. Bronston did not bite. She had had her fill of guilt trips. She didn't choose to take any more. Her convenience "no" was the no of a woman foresighted enough to see that her familial responsibilities did not obligate her to ignore her personal needs. She had a right to enjoy the pause that refreshes. She owed it to herself to take time out to read an adult book for a change, rather than the fairy tales she frequently read her child. It was important for her sanity to set aside those personal moments for relaxing, chatting with a friend, shopping, or just doing nothing. She was a mother and a woman both. To be only one and not the other would be to be nothing at all.

Adults who devote all of their time and energy to enlarging their children's lives diminish their own. The all work and no play habit wears them out emotionally. Neither the grown-up nor those growing up are well served. Unhappy parents cannot rear happy children. Adult exhaustion leads to irritation, and inevitably, to the feeling of being put upon. Resentment and regret become the by-products of such lopsided give-and-take between parent and child. Unfortunately, many adults do not realize this. They cling to the belief that they owe total devotion to their offspring. Most feel certain that they will be well rewarded for their sacrifice. They are wrong. Other men and women explain that their joy is in the giving, they insist that they expect no other reward for their complete selflessness than to see their children live happy, healthy, productive lives. These parents are wrong, too. The need for gratitude, appreciation, and esteem is human, natural, and universal. No matter how genuinely or generously a parent gives to a child, there is always an expectation of return. Whether expressed or subconscious, a giver always expects some kind of compensation. Whenever he makes a deposit, he feels entitled to a return.

"I wonder if the kind of music where the words make sense will ever come back again!" Uncle Fred asked his wife, jokingly.

"Or, where the words are simple and sweet, not all sexually suggestive," she added with more seriousness.

"I don't see what the devil the kids see in that punk rock, anyway. It's meaningless, crude, and talk about loud . . . in a few minutes it can puncture an ear drum," her husband agreed.

"How right you are," his wife said. "Lucky you only promised to drive Abby to the concert rather than take her."

"Take her? . . . I was even thinking of parking three blocks away to let her off, so I wouldn't have to hear all those screaming, screeching kids pushing to get in the place," he joked.

When eleven-year-old Abby suddenly walked into the room, the kidding came to an end. She looked distraught.

"What's the matter?" Uncle Fred asked anxiously.

"Cousin Ronnie's sick, and he can't go with me to the stadium today. I tried to get somebody else, but even with offering them a free ticket, I can't find anyone," she groaned. "Everybody old enough works Saturday afternoons or something."

"So . . . you'll go alone," suggested Aunt Lois. Uncle Fred will drop you off, see that you get into the place safely, and he'll be waiting for you right by the River Street exit when the show is over."

"I can't," Abby said dejectedly. "Because of all

190

the beer drinking and pot smoking they've had at other concerts, you have to be eighteen to get in, or you have to be accompanied by an adult."

"Gee, I'm sorry," Uncle Fred said sympathetically. "I know how much you've been waiting for this group to come to town."

"Uncle Fred!" Abby insisted pathetically. "You've just got to take me . . . you can use Ronnie's ticket. Please . . . I'll do anything if you will."

The look on his niece's face made Fred Green wince. How could he refuse her?

"I'm . . . I'm sorry, Ab . . . but I have to say NO!"

"Why?" her voice rose tearfully.

"Because I'm not interested in punk rock music. It's too loud . . . and too . . . well, it just doesn't suit my taste."

"But you don't have to like the Shotguns to go with me. Just come and sit there with me."

"No, I can't," Uncle Fred replied. "If I don't enjoy that kind of music—and I don't—it doesn't make sense for me to waste my Saturday afternoon with it, does it?"

"But . . . I like their music . . . I love their songs. How will I get to hear them?"

Her uncle thought for a moment. "You and I will drive over to the stadium early. The show has been a sellout for weeks, so there's no question about your being able to get your money back for the tickets. But we won't even try to do that until we've looked over the crowd. Maybe there'll be someone there you or I know who would take you in with them. Aunt Lois and I know a lot of people in town, so there's a real chance we'll see someone. But if we don't, Abby . . . no begging, no whining, no sulking. The tickets get returned . . . because I have no interest in spending the day listening to rock music.

The point of no return between adult and child frequently can be avoided. Intelligent use of the convenience "no" can find an alternate solution or compromise. Without compromising the interests and predispositions of the adult, a counter offer is sometimes possible. But not always! To a preschooler, it may take the form of postponement or redirection. "I can't play with you now, but you can help me put the groceries away." "My throat is getting sore from reading this book over and over. I'll turn the pages while you look at the pictures and tell me the story."

The school-aged child is advised to use her legs rather than insist upon a ride when it is inconvenient for the adult; she is directed to practice her part in the play with another sibling or a friend, rather than bother Grandmother when she's relaxing. Similarly, the teenager is instructed to meet with his classmate to study, rather than tie up the telephone. Or, he may be asked to keep a checklist of requirements for his learners permit so that Dad doesn't have to be bothered taking care of them one at a time on days inconvenient for him. Whenever the wants of the child *and* the wishes of the adult are acknowledged, accepted as valid, and appreciated, the possibility for accommodation is increased. Uncle Fred's proposal was a step in that direction. He appreciated Abby's situation and understood the intensity of her desire to attend the concert. He was more than willing to satisfy his niece if he could, as long as he did not have to sacrifice his own freedom of choice.

The choice of the convenience "no" should not be motivated by an adult's desire to show the child "just who is boss around here." Nor is it meant to arbitrarily prohibit youngsters from getting what they want. The main purpose is to legitimatize the adult's option for self-actualization outside the parental role. Men and women should not feel guilty when they have to refuse or postpone the wishes of their children. They should not feel they are being selfish on the occasions when they consider their own needs first. Nor should boys or girls feel unloved or resentful when decisions are made on the basis of their parents' convenience. The convenience "no" should help children and parents learn to accept the fact that men and women have a right to life, liberty, and the pursuit of happiness with their offspring as well as separate and apart from them.

"Boy, if that's what you call fair!" eight-year-old Harry shouted. "You won't let me watch TV because you say it's a big waste . . . but you watch it all the time."

"I'm older than you,"the boy's foster parent explained patiently.

"Then you should be smarter . . . smart enough not to do things you say aren't good to do," the boy shot back flippantly.

"I've worked hard all day," Mr. Gordon tried to explain. "I need to—well, you wouldn't understand Harry—but to unwind. You've still got your homework to do. Anyway . . . the show I'm watching isn't the kind a little boy should see. You can learn a lot better things from your books."

"Books stink!" Harry retorted. "And so do you, for being so mean. They let me watch all the television I wanted anytime I wanted to in the other home I lived in. They didn't never say 'No, you can't.' "

Restricting Harry from seeing life and death whiz by in black and white or living color demanded strong conviction. Most parents find it more convenient to let the plug-in-drug keep youngsters satisfied. Television is the cheapest baby-sitter in town. It not only keeps boys and girls out of mom's and dad's hair, it doesn't raid the refrigerator or need a ride home. Harry's father felt uncomfortable allowing the boy to watch the kind of program that should be reserved for adults. He used the convenience "no," but with a great deal of guilt. "In one way, the boy is right," Mr. Gordon thought. "If I sit around watching the tube, how can I insist he shouldn't?" Even the fathers and mothers who spend limitless time in an activity such as watching television have the right to set limits for their children. Boys and girls are not adults. What is good for grown-ups is often totally inappropriate for children. Extensive television watching is one such activity. By the time a person has reached adulthood, he or she is, for the most part, formed in his tastes, values, and habits. Parents have a right to use TV as they choose—as a relaxant, a source of information, a form of entertainment. Like Mr. Gordon, many people use it to unwind and to escape into other times, places, and life-styles.

Whatever the purpose, most adults are capable of differentiating between reality and what appears on the screen. Children are not! Allowed to sit as silent spectators, they are channeled into a seeing-is-believing mind-set. The aggressive behavior, inappropriate speech, and unattainable expectations projected on TV are mistaken for the real thing. Harry's father understood that his foster son was still in the most formative years of his life; his habits and values were being formed. Mr. Gordon's convenience "no" had a dual purpose: It suited his own recreational needs, and it protected Harry from the harm of overexposure.

Overexposure to the convenience "no," like overexposure to television, is harmful. Parents who are excessively self-centered teach their children to be selfish. "Monkey see, monkey do"; these youngsters do only what is fun or convenient for them. They shirk all responsibilities which are unpleasant or unprofitable. They do not mature from ego-centered human beings to more other-centered, humane beings. Both their social and emotional growth is retarded by too many convenience "no's" unfairly imposed on them. Prevented from normal exploring and experimenting, these children are not allowed to learn by doing, or through making their own mistakes. Their self-image is diminished, also.

"Norman," the kindergarten teacher insisted. "Now, you must have a last name. All the other boys and girls in the class have told me theirs."
"Nope. I'm just Norman," he whispered shyly.
Searching for some way to stimulate the boy's understanding, the teacher said, "Well, let's pretend you and two other boys named Norman are playing in your backyard. Your mother wanted you to come in for dinner, but she didn't want the other two Normans to think she was calling them. What would she call out to you to let you know that you were the Norman she wanted?"
The boy hesitated.
"Would she call, Norman Brown! . . . Norman Jonston! or Norman what?"
Now the kindergartener's face brightened. "My other name is NO. That's what Mommy always calls out to me . . . NORMAN, NO . . . NORMAN, NO."

There are Norman and Norma No's of all ages. "Norman, no . . . don't touch that." "Norma, no . . . don't bother me." These children live at and for the convenience of their parents, in the same way that some adults exist solely for the sake of their children. Both kinds of parent-child relationships are out of balance. They are inadequately constructed. Neither is capable of supporting a solid, satisfying interaction between parent and child. Respect and trust do not develop in a relationship where one person does all the giving and the other all the taking. The convenience "no" is a good restraint to use when used fairly . . . but too much of anything, even a good thing, becomes a bad thing. Particularly serious damage

195

is done to boys and girls who are always conveniently ignored by their parents. These men and women find it a bother to have to take the time to care for their children, to discipline them, to teach them the difference between right and wrong.

"Well, don't ask me why I'm here," the young boy said to the pastor. "I told Jill you couldn't do anything for me . . . that I didn't need anybody to do anything for me, but she asked me to see you so . . . here's looking at you," Cliff said flippantly.

"Well . . . I'm glad you came," the older man said. "Just now, I'm not sure there are any job leads I can give you, but let's talk . . . let me get to know you." As Reverend Cooper spoke, his eyes surveyed Cliff. He was wearing skin-tight blue jeans, chrome-rimmed sunglasses, and the wisps of a scraggly beard. His shoulder-length hair was knotted behind his ears in a ponytail. His short leather boots were pointed at the toe and run down at the heels, but all five foot seven inches of him walked tall and tough. Why not? Hadn't he experienced, experimented, explored everything there was to examine in his short seventeen years of life: drugs; sex, normal and kinky; work, legal and illegal. Nobody could control or con him. Nobody could tell him anything because he already knew it.

"Jill's a very fine young woman," the pastor began hesitatingly. "Her third grade class is really devoted to her."

"Well . . . anybody that can keep kids coming to Sunday School has got to be something special," Cliff agreed. "Nobody could get me to go."

"Oh," Reverend Cooper replied. "How old were you when you stopped?"

"About eight. I was in the third grade, I think," Cliff answered.

"Was your mother an active church member?"

"I don't think so, but that wouldn't have mattered; she let me do whatever I wanted to."

"When you were such a young child, she let you do whatever you wanted to?" the pastor asked in surprise.

"Sure . . . I did whatever I wanted . . . went where I wanted . . . for as far back as I can remember. I stayed out as late as I wanted . . . things like that," the boy answered.

The Reverend seemed unprepared for this kind of confession.

"You mean there was no adult at home who established rules for you . . . bedtime rules, homework obligations, mealtime regulation?"

"Like I told Jill . . . me and Mom and my older brother, we all lived together, ya know. I picked up a lot from him, even though he wasn't around too much, really. Anyway, I guess my mom figured I was smart for a little kid. She trusted me to take care of myself, and I did. Mealtimes were when I was hungry. There was always something around to eat if she wasn't home . . . something in the fridge or on the stove. I wasn't a baby, ya know."

"Tell me, Cliff," the pastor seemed suddenly quiet. "Are you trying to tell me that the reason your mother didn't impose any rules on you . . . didn't limit what you did or didn't do, was because she thought you were big enough to be trusted?"

"Sure," he shot back. "That's the way it was. She trusted me. She knew I didn't need anybody babying me and running things for me."

The religious leader answered nothing. Finally, he said, "You call it trust, Cliff, but think back, if you can . . . to how it seemed to you when you were ten or eleven. Did your mother's leaving you

197

on your own seem like a compliment or benefit, then? Did it make you feel big and strong and sure of yourself? Were you really glad that she left you alone . . . to do your own thing, as they say?"

Cliff's eyes narrowed. The suave, cocky look with which he entered the study slowly disappeared. He seemed suddenly childish and vulnerable.

"I . . . guess . . . back then, when she wasn't around much . . . when everything I did was OK . . . as long as I didn't bother her . . . well, back then, Reverend, I guess I felt that . . . she didn't give a damn about me," Cliff sighed.

No restriction, or lack of restriction, placed on a child should make him feel his parent doesn't give a damn. In the give-and-take between the two, caring, one for the other, should be the link that binds them. Should this link be missing, there is little to hold them together. Every "no" which is said to a child should communicate concern, acceptance, and affection for him. Even when his behavior is disliked, he must know he is still liked. The fairness, firmness, and agreeability with which an instruction is given is as important as the content of the message itself. How willingly boys and girls obey directions and accept limitations is closely related to how much respect they have for the person giving them. Respect builds trust, and trust obedience. Men and women skillful enough to apply the convenience "no" sensibly and sensitively do not control children's lives; they structure them. They build confidence in the child, not confusion. In saying "no," parents show they care enough to give the very best to both their children and themselves.

1. Parents are not only mothers and fathers, they are people. They have individual needs and wants which require recognition.

2. Children's wants and the wishes of adults sometimes conflict. Fair, firm, agreeable, and guiltless use of the convenience "no" allows parents to give their preferences priority.

3. A family relationship based on giving the child everything he wants on a silver platter soon tarnishes. Things which come easily are easily taken for granted.

4. Excessive use of the convenience "no" weakens the parent-child relationship as much as failure to use it. Men and women who consider no one but themselves rear inconsiderate children.

5. Not only how frequently a restraint is applied, but how it is done and by whom determines its effectiveness. If there is real caring between adults and children, usually it is convenient for them to consider one another.

11.

THE THREE "NO'S" THAT HARM

There was a little girl, and she had a little curl
Right in the middle of her forehead.
When she was good, she was very, very good,
And when she was bad, she was horrid.

Use of the word, "no" with children can be very, very good for them—or it can be horrid. The lifesaving "no," the challenge "no," the character-building "no," and the convenience "no" give youngsters the structure they need. Fairly, firmly, consistently, and caringly, these "no's" improve their physical, social, emotional, and spiritual growth. Three other "no's" often said to boys and girls produce negative results. Youngsters are belittled and frightened by them. "No, I don't love you," "No, you're not capable," and "No, I won't listen to you," are words that should never be said to children.

"Mom, I just don't feel good enough to go to school, today," Sonny insisted. "My throat feels sore and . . . I dunno . . . I don't feel good."

Mrs. Gregory looked at her nine-year-old son suspiciously. She went over to him and felt his forehead. "You're cool as a cucumber," she said. "You couldn't be *that* sick."

"But it hurts . . . I . . ."

"I don't want to hear another word about it. Just get up, get dressed, and get to school," his mother insisted.

"But honest, Mom, I'm not making it up . . . my head feels . . ."

"I'm not listening, young man. I'm not paying one bit of attention to your crybabying. If I stayed home from work every time I didn't feel like getting up and going . . . or whenever my stomach felt a little upset, I'd never be able to keep a job. The subject is closed," she declared, as she turned to leave the room.

Sonny looked like he was about to cry.

"If you don't feel any better once you're at school, let the nurse take a look at you," Mother offered.

"But can't I just stay home for a little while and maybe go in late, when I feel better?" her son pleaded.

"No, you can't! Now don't get me angry. Get up and get ready for school without saying one more word about it."

Many parents just don't want to hear about it when children say they're sick. The adults object to bellyaching and complaining. Some suspect the kids are only pretending to be ill so they can miss school. Others believe children ought to be raised in a tough enough manner to grin and bear a stomach pain, runny nose, or headache. In many families, boys and girls are browbeaten into keeping their troubles to themselves. Young children in particular are shamed and ridiculed into keeping a stiff upper lip. "Now stop that. Big boys don't cry!" they are admonished. "Act your age, young lady. You're too old to let a little thing like *that* upset you!" Older children are silenced sternly by sarcasm and made to feel guilty for their troubles. "If you think you feel lousy, let me tell you about *my* problems," Mother challenges the preadolescent. "Can't you see you're wasting my time with all your 'feeling sorry for yourself.'" "I've got a hell of a lot more important things to do than sit around here listening to you bitch," Father growls to his teenager.

Whether it is said in ridicule or anger, the "No, I won't listen" forces children to keep their troubles to themselves. Unfortunately, those in trouble don't get out of it by remaining silent. To expect a child of any age to suffer in silence is expecting too much. And, it is dangerous! The child who is unable to get his problems off his chest and onto his tongue has little chance of getting them out of his way. No problem can be seen clearly unless it is out in the open. Resolving whatever is wrong is impossible unless the full scope of the youngster's concerns have been voiced. Only when both child and parent understand the distress and its source can the resulting pain and suffering be alleviated. The best first-aid that a parent can give a child in distress is the simple relief of allowing him to share his burden with someone. The child's anxiety is then relieved. He no longer has to hide his feelings and be eaten up inside by pent-up fear and discomfort.

Sonny's mother did nothing to ease her son's discomfort. Her actions were hasty and insensitive. She showed neither sympathy for nor trust in him. The nine-year-old needed time to explain how he felt, but she refused to give it. He deserved the respect of being both "seen and heard." Even if afterward, he was sent to school anyway, the listening would not have been wasted. Mother might have learned enough to decide whether to give him an aspirin, some cough syrup, or a kiss to make him feel better. Sonny would have learned that Mom was interested in what he had to say. The boy would have gained assurance that Mom could be relied upon at least to listen when he needed her.

Just because parents listen to children's complaints does not mean that they encourage "crybabying;" nor does listening increase the chances that a child will become a chronic complainer because he enjoys the attention he gets. The act of listening is a neutral one—it neither condemns nor condones. Listening to what children have to say allows parents to better evaluate the seriousness of the complaint. By knowing everything the youngster can tell them, parents have more information to go on when deciding whether it is necessary to investigate his condition further. Should a doctor be called? Are there tensions in the family or at school which are causing the distress?

Boys and girls who are allowed to express their feelings enjoy more prompt relief. The freedom to complain is a therapeutic one. It should not be denied. Pain and "just not feeling good" are the body's signals that something is wrong. Boys and girls must feel free to tell someone they can trust whenever their built-in warning system flashes its red light. If they do not, a minor irritation can fester, become inflamed, and develop into a serious situation.

Michael Kent Esquire was totally unprepared for what the truant officer was saying to him. "Judge, I certainly believe you when you tell me you thought your son was in school all last week . . . but the fact is—he wasn't."

"Well, where was he?" Judge Kent asked excitedly.

"I figure he was hanging out on the streets like a

204

lot of them kids do . . . or maybe he was in and out of a movie or two. You'd be surprised, Your Honor, if I told you how many junior high school kids skip school each day. Absenteeism is a whale of a problem, not only in this town but everywhere!"

"But last week was like any other week; we got up, had breakfast, and then I dropped Mike off at school on my way to the courthouse."

"Well, what I'm saying is, he never made it *into* school."

"Are they sure? I mean, does the teacher really know him?—we've only lived in this neighborhood a month. Maybe she has him mixed up with another boy . . . you know those teachers have eight classes a day, and maybe her records . . ." Judge Kent stammered.

"Michael Kent, Jr., was not in school all last week, sir, no mistake about it," the truant officer emphasized, checking his notebook.

"Well, I'll tell you one thing! He'll be in school from now on, if . . . I have to take him through the door myself, and tie him to his desk," the father promised.

Soon after the truant officer left, twelve-year-old Michael returned from the soccer game.

"Sit right down here!" his father ordered briskly. "Why did you skip school all last week?"

The boy's face reddened. His lips quivered.

"Answer me!" his father ordered more forcefully.

"None of those kids like me. I'm new around here, so I get all the teasing and elbowing and wisecracks, and my lunch box grabbed away from me . . . I hate them!"

"Well, is that any reason not to go to school and learn something so you can BE somebody? Just ig-

205

nore them," his father replied more calmly. "Besides, why didn't you tell your teacher? Why didn't you tell me, instead of being truant?"

"I DID," his son shouted. "I tried to tell you lots of times . . . but you wouldn't listen. Last week I told you Jack Jeffreys called me a nigger, but you said, 'Forget it. I don't want to hear any of that garbage—*you* know who you are!' Before that, I tried to tell you the work was too hard, because in the other school I never learned any algebra, but you said, 'No, I won't listen to that excuse—study harder, or get more help from the teacher' . . . I couldn't do the work, and I hate those kids, and I tried to tell you, but you wouldn't listen," Mike sobbed.

Whether a child's aches and pains are physical or emotional, they hurt just the same. Peers who torment, dreams that frighten, or choices that confuse can be even more uncomfortable than the earaches, sore throats, and runny noses that are so much a normal part of growing up. Biologically and psychologically, misery loves company. The company that a miserable child wants is adult company. Parental companionship provides support and security. Children are more at ease when they know that someone else knows how they feel. Boys and girls gain confidence when they feel somebody else cares—someone big enough and wise enough to help make things better. Judge Kent was not wise enough to help make things better. He was not wise enough to pay attention to the things his son tried to tell him. Some things, he unthinkingly ignored. Others, he curtly sloughed off as undeserving of his time. Had he listened more carefully, he would have gotten Mike's cues, and he would then have known enough to act on them. Instead, his inattention and inaction played a major part in the boy's becoming truant.

Boys and girls of every age experience alienation and anger.

Many feel they are alone and afraid in a world they never made. Children who are able to share their confusions with adults find the environment more predictable and friendly. They sense that they have an ally who understands them and will support them. Parents who stop, look, and listen to what is burdening a child help to lighten his load. Frequently, they stop the trouble before it begins.

"Mommy, Mommy, there's a big bear in my room," Dottie cried out in the night. "He's trying to get me—to eat me up."

Awakened from a deep sleep, Mother rushed into her daughter's room. Not in full control of her thoughts or motions, she stubbed her toe, tripping over the dollhouse that had not been put away. "Damn it! What do you mean a bear?" Mrs. Sandler challenged, as she switched on the light. "There's no bear in here; you were dreaming!"

The six-year-old looked around the room anxiously; "I saw it," she insisted. "A black grizzly bear almost in my room . . . coming right in the window."

"There was no bear," Mother insisted. "You were dreaming . . . now I'm very tired; I'm going to tuck you in and you go back to sleep."

"But the bear!" the little girl began.

"Bears do not live in this part of the country! Besides, can't you see that the window is too small for any bear to crawl through? Now go to sleep! I don't want to hear another word out of you about bears, do you hear me?"

One of the most important things parents should listen to are children's fears. Like adult fears, they are of two types: rational and irrational. Both are equally painful. Ignoring either one is dangerous. Rational fears are those associated with immediate and real dangers. A speeding car bearing down on a child induces normal fear. Being caught cheating in class also causes fear, fear of the consequences. Irrational or imaginary fears are more properly called anxieties. A child is afraid to cross a street because he fears that a car, not even in sight, may hit him. A boy refuses to wear his new wristwatch outside the house, because he is afraid of losing it. The normality or abnormality of fears is determined by their basis in reality and by the degree of anxiety the child experiences. Sometimes the line between the two is very thin.

Real or imaginary, whatever frightens, perplexes, or captures the fancy of a child should be heard and heeded. When Dottie cried out anxiously in the night, she needed to be reassured with tender loving listening. Mrs. Sandler should have held her daughter and encouraged her to tell her about what scared her. Shutting Dottie up left all the fear and confusion still churning within her. Equally unsupportive and futile was Mother's attempt to win the battle of logic with the little girl. Whether bears only inhabited the woods or were too large to squeeze through a small bedroom window mattered little to Dottie. That level of reasoning was beyond the level of her fears. What mattered was what was real to the frightened child at that moment, not what was factually correct. Until she talked out her fantasy, she had no room in her mind for reality.

Distressed children are not comforted by adult logic unless it is preceded by adult listening. Parents who listen provide children with an audience upon whom they may expend the full brunt of their fear and confusion. Only when a child's misgivings are given a chance to be aired in a reassuring atmosphere can they be replaced by the supportive explanations and remedies parents may provide.

Attentive and supportive listening not only provides emotional security for boys and girls, it also benefits them socially and intellectually.

"No, I can't stop now and listen to you, Jody. I

have to get supper ready . . . why don't you go watch television!"

"Can't you wait until Daddy comes home, George; I can't sit here all day while you tell me about the story you read in school."

More and more parents seem preoccupied with the rat race of their own existence. They don't know how to slow down long enough to listen to children . . . *really* listen! Perhaps they do not understand the importance of occasionally adapting themselves to their child's pace. Listening to what children have to say is a valuable learning tool for both grown-ups and those growing up. Taking time out to hear what preschoolers and first and second graders have to say is particularly important. Talking with adults gives children the opportunity to translate what they hear and think into the words we speak. They get important practice in putting words together in sentences, and increase their vocabulary. They learn many other skills of verbal communication as well. Boys and girls are required to organize their thoughts better and express their ideas in logical, sequential order. Both their tongues and their brains are given good exercise when they are allowed to speak up. A child's readiness to read is also greatly aided. The more children speak, the larger the vocabulary they develop. Boys and girls learn to pronounce words more accurately. They also gain skill in developing their simple one- or two-word sentences ("Doggy lost." "Mommy look.") into compound and complex ones ("My Doggy got lost, but I found him." "Mommy, look at me when I jump."). The larger their vocabulary, the clearer their pronunciation, and the more variety in sentence structure that children bring to the reading process, the better. Reading is visual speech. The more familiar and comfortable boys and girls are with the spoken word, the more prepared they are to understand it in its written form.

No matter how old a child is, practice makes his power of speech more perfect. Increased vocabulary, improved diction, and better organization of thought result when preadolescents and teenagers know they are welcome to speak up. As long as the environment is not threatening, children will talk whenever given the chance. What they talk about gives parents the opportunity to gain valuable information for guiding them.

"Mom, I . . . ya know . . . well, ah, Margo, well . . . she was held back in school so she's fourteen already . . ."

"Yes, I think I know who you mean," Mother responded with interest.

"Well . . . she's a flirt . . . I mean she already goes around with all those guys in the twelfth grade."

"Oh, does she?" Mrs. Cooper replied nonjudgmentally.

"Yeah, and a . . . she told me—I mean . . . her mother took her to be fitted for something . . . I think they call it a diaphragm—it's so she can't have a baby. She said the pill is dangerous cause you can get a lot of bad reactions or something."

The reaction parents have after listening to children is as important as their willingness to listen. "No, I won't listen" should never be said to restrict a child from expressing himself. Nor should it be used to dismiss what the child says once he's had his say. Listening leads to liveliness in the communication between adult and child. It also helps close the generation gap between adult and child. Normal children of every age are inquisitive and interested, but only partially informed. There are huge gaps between what they think they know and the knowledge they actually possess. The depth of information boys and girls have is much more shallow than the number of things about which they have something to say.

Children actually want to know, need to know, and have a

right to know the answers to questions affecting their growth and development. By carefully listening to them, men and women can become aware of the questions with which children are grappling. Parents who fully understand the questions are in a better position to give considered answers. Mrs. Cooper's teenage daughter was questioning her about human sexuality. She wanted her mother to know what was going on in the peer group. Sharing this made the child feel safer. The teenager also wanted Mom to talk to her about sex, but she didn't feel like just coming out and bluntly asking.

One of the most crucial and difficult responsibilities of parenthood is providing honest, thorough sex guidance to children. Counseling against the abuse of drugs and alcohol is equally important. As children mature and enter new stages of life, they need to be prepared for what comes next. Some parents deny them this necessary preparation. Many adults never grew up enough themselves to maturely face the facts of life with their children. These men and women turn their backs on their responsibility to provide guidelines for their children on the matter of sex and drugs. Some nervously answer young children's queries with, "You're too young to know about that," or "Let's talk about that later." Listening to children enables parents to tell when that "later" has arrived. Whether the questions concern school, sex, crime, or any vice or virtue, they should be answered. Adults who avoid responding to boys' and girls' questions are guilty of child neglect. If Mrs. Cooper had not been able to honestly and thoroughly discuss human sexuality with her daughter, the girl would have had no other choice but to take her questions to the street. Like many other children, she would pick up raw sewage from the gutter of smut magazines and pornographic movies. The dirty jokes and half-truths provided by peers would be her best source of information.

Listening attentively and answering supportively is an important parental responsibility. To say, "No, I won't listen" is irresponsible and dangerous. To the child, growing up is complex and confusing. Real and imagined problems continually beset boys and girls. The small child who is afraid to venture far from home because he imagines someone may beat him up—the youngster who doesn't want to close her eyes at night because she is afraid she'll die in her sleep like Grandpa did— both need parents to stop, look, and listen to them. When a child moves from one neighborhood to another, loses the companionship of mother or father through divorce or death, or lives in a home disrupted by alcoholism, abuse, or chronic economic problems, he has troubles to which someone must lend an ear. School worries, peer pressures, human sexual drives, and the need to become independent and self-disciplined present confusion for all boys and girls. Children feel desperately alone when they have only themselves to talk to.

There can be no strength in a parent-child relationship when girls and boys are treated like silent partners. A solid relationship is based upon the following guidelines.

1. Children should be seen and "heard out." They have real and imagined fears, confusions, and questions to which adults ought to lend an ear.

2. The amount and kind of listening parents do shows whether they really respect the freedom of speech of those growing up. Adults who are good listeners avoid allowing a child to feel that his thoughts are boring, immature, or wasteful of adult time. Listening without interruption, looking directly and sensitively at the child speaking, and seriously thinking about how to help him are attitudes which comprise good parent-listening skills.

3. Men and women who pay attention to their child, positively affect his emotional, social, and intellectual growth. Children are more at ease and more motivated to resolve their difficulties when they know somebody else is aware of how they feel—somebody big enough and wise enough to help them. Important, too, is the

companionship provided by parents who give their undivided attention to the child needing to be heard. Mother's helpful ideas, Dad's understanding attitude, Uncle Joe's pat on the back, all provide a warm social climate of trust and respect. Intellectually, the child encouraged to speak and share his thoughts develops important communication skills. He learns to organize his thoughts and present them accurately. Through confident use, the child's vocabulary, sentence structure and clarity of pronunciation improves. Practice makes boys and girls not only more perfect in their speaking, but also in their reading.

"No, you're not capable" (of doing that) is another injurious restraint to children. Boys and girls exposed to this kind of "no" inevitably see themselves as inadequate and inferior. Their self-actualization is retarded. The lack of faith adults have in them is communicated in many ways. Through the teacher's body language, father's attitude, and mother's action, the child is reminded of his shortcomings. Nonverbal messages speak as loudly as the words used to let the child know he's not good enough. When a child is intentionally or inadvertently denied an adult's confidence and respect, he cannot measure up to the brightest and the best that is within him.

"Now, honey, put that book away; it's too hard for you!" Mother warned protectively.

"But I like it; it's about space ships," nine-year-old Kurt replied, taking a thick book from the library shelf toward the checkout desk.

"You won't be able to read it. Find an easier one." Mother insisted.

"I can read it," Kurt replied.

"There are plenty of other books here! How about this nice one on cowboys. It looks like it doesn't have too many hard words and the print is larger."

"But, Mom, I want this one about outer space."

"Then find an easier one like it. It's no sense lugging that big book home when you won't be able to read it!" Mother insisted.

"All the other kids in my class read it, and they said it was cool."

"But they're not you," his mother replied in a more irritated voice. "You know you don't read as well as they do. Listen to me, I know you won't be able to read a book that difficult."

"Dad, why won't you let me help you fix the garage door today?"

"Because, I want to do it alone!"

"Please can't I do something with you?"

"Not today, Craig. I've got a lot of things to do, and it slows me up when you help. I have to keep explaining what to do and . . ."

"Please, Dad, I'll be faster. I could hand you the nails or hammer some or . . ."

"Look, I said no! Last week you were fast, and you spilled the whole box of nails all over the floor. Remember how long it took me to find them. I could have driven out of the garage and punctured a tire. I just don't have the time to waste . . . now, you can't hang around here today, Craig," Father said firmly. "Besides, you can have a lot more fun at the playground. Go find somebody to shoot baskets with, why don't you?"

For the child who is made to feel incompetent shooting baskets is not much fun. He may be slow in reading, slow in following directions, or slow in throwing a ball, but he is quick to catch on to how adults feel about him. Mom and Dad think he can't do anything right. They don't even trust him to try. Deep inside, the youngster feels hurt, angry, humiliated, helpless. Even if he should understand that mother and father are trying to protect him from failure, his frustration remains. The adult's motivation doesn't change anything. What is, is! He is *inferior*.

Despite the injurious backlash of their protectiveness, many parents illogically prevent boys and girls from doing what they want to do—and what they may be perfectly capable of doing. Some adults mistakenly believe that it is better to keep children from trying something than to risk letting them fail. Another group of erring men and women are not at all concerned with the child's saving face; their only concern is with saving their own time. Both the parents who try to serve as buffers and those who protect only themselves hinder the emotional and social growth of their children. To a child, parents are the most important people in his life. They are his security blanket and his role model. When mother or father brand a child as incapable, the label sticks. Often the parents are committing a "truth in packaging" fraud. Their youngster is not as helpless or hopeless as they claim he is. Nevertheless, the child sees himself as his mother and father see him. He measures his worth on their scale. Were he allowed to do what he thinks he can do, he might surprise them. Were he encouraged to try to do the best he can, he would probably do better than he expected. But Mother's prejudgments and Dad's inflexibility prevent the child from giving his best to anything. Dejected, Craig goes to see if the "butterfingers" that can't hold onto nails can at least toss a ball through a hoop correctly. Kurt, the poor reader, takes the easier book about cowboys and wonders why he can't be like the other kids. What each child learns from his experience is more emphatic than any personal failure.

Children of all ages ought to gain the confidence which comes from doing things for themselves. Unless parents give them a chance, boys and girls cannot accomplish anything.

> "Here, Carla, let Mommy do that! I'll make your bed. I'm bigger, so I can make it faster and neater than you, sweetheart."

> "For heaven's sakes! Give me the cloth, Juan!

You're not helping to wipe the dust off the shelf, you're spreading it around all over the place."

"That's all right, Shirley! Granny knows you had a lot of toys to put away. You just get into bed, and I'll straighten up the mess for you!"

"Look, Gordon, you didn't do what I told you to. You didn't clean the cat's water bowl before you filled it. See all the dirt in the bottom. Give it to me. I guess the only way anything is going to be done right around here is if *I* do it!"

Large numbers of three-, four- and five-year-olds have nothing to do. They are jobless. The adults in their lives do everything for them. Mother finds it faster to pick up after the child than encourage him to do his own dirty work. Parents accept whatever poor effort a youngster applies to a task just to avoid his negativism or screaming when corrected. Showing a child the right way to do something and insisting he do it does not occur to these parents. Adults are forced to work overtime, but the boys and girls are the ones who get shortchanged. Youngsters who do nothing, learn nothing. When parents do everything for children, they promote a bad habit: idleness! Children lack the inclination to test their own abilities. They have no reason to try and no opportunity to succeed. Without successful experiences to rely upon, youngsters do not build the courage to trust their own capabilities.

Regardless of how young a child is, he needs to experience success. Attaining success depends not only upon his actual ability, but upon whether or not adults give him a chance to show what he knows, and can do. From preschooler through the teenage years, children should learn by doing. Each and every child has some degree of capability. Usually he has a great deal more potential than parents credit him with. Whether it is baking a cake, washing the family car, "baby-sitting" or raising his science grade from D to C, a child needs to have something to do and something to look forward to.

Whether he does something well, better than he did before, or merely gives it a good try, he should be able to look forward to some recognition. By doing things for himself, a child gains greater competence and confidence. His sense of responsibility, pride, and self-mastery, develop when, through his trials and errors, he is able to "make the grade."

"It's your decision, Mrs. Silverstein, but if you ask me, Stuart should remain in the first grade next year. I think he probably entered school when he was too young," the teacher added. "But that's water over the dam now. The point is, he's just not as socially mature as his classmates. He's still reading at the primer level, too. Another year here will give him the headstart he needs to succeed in school."

"Please don't misunderstand, Ms. McCarthy. It isn't that I don't trust your judgment," Stuart's mother replied. "My concern is, how will my son feel about being left back? What about the friendships he's made?"

"Oh, I'm sure he'll be able to make new friends if he tries," the teacher replied.

When children don't succeed in school, they are exposed to a painful experience. The boy or girl required to repeat a grade generally becomes the oldest and biggest pupil in the class. He sticks out like a sore thumb, physically and scholastically. Frequently, he is ridiculed by peers as "the dummy" or "the retard." Even an insensitive teacher can make him feel like a failure. The repeater never fails to hear her impatient sighs when he struggles through "reading aloud." He sees her uplifted eyebrows and pursed lips when he asks a question that she thinks he ought to be able to answer himself. As the teacher turns away toward another classmate when he comes to her desk for help, the boy knows where he stands . . . not anywhere near the head of the class!

The lesson learned by the child who is "pushed ahead" to

the next grade, rather than left back, may be equally demoralizing. Without strong academic and emotional support, he finds the classwork "way over his head." No matter how hard he struggles, he can't rise and shine. Not only the things classmates say to him, but the marks the teacher gives are degrading.

To make the grade (no matter which one seems the better choice) a youngster requires a teacher who can adapt the curriculum to him, rather than the other way around. Each boy or girl is a unique human being. He possesses needs and wants both similar to, and strikingly different from, those of his classmates. Young people function best under the leadership of adults who try to learn how the child feels in a given situation and help him to be more at ease. Helping children to understand that making mistakes is a normal part of living and learning provides a solid base for the kind of security a child needs in order to learn. When adults respect the child as he is, wherever he is, they build the youngster's faith in himself and his trust in adult guidance. Teachers and parents who do not handle children with such care create social and emotional failures.

Failure is an emotional boomerang. The danger lies in its tendency to always come back. Each time the child's inadequacies are pointed out to him, he is hit in a most vulnerable spot—his ego. The blow diminishes the youngster's feeling of self-worth. Seeing himself as inept at reading, subtracting, or behaving, the child becomes a victim of the self-fulfilling prophecy: He reads, subtracts, and behaves poorly. When teachers, parents, or peers communicate that a child is incapable, he sees himself through their eyes. Seeing is believing. Believing he cannot succeed, the child gives up trying. He neglects to practice the tasks which would perfect his capability. Failure to practice and learn from his mistakes dooms the child to remain unskilled. The actual lack of success which results from never trying completes the vicious cycle of failure for him. The child's poor spelling, multiplication, or speaking serves as proof positive to him, and to the adults who labeled him incapable, that their judgment was correct.

Adults who verbally or nonverbally tell a child, "No, you're not capable" make him a psychological cripple. Boys and girls whose minds have been set to see themselves as incompetent, act accordingly. They develop a fail-safe method against succeeding.

Emily wasn't much of a success at anything, but she plugged away at it anyway. Her school days were rarely brightened by the teacher's warm smile or praise. At home, her mother's method of pushing and pressuring her to do better was to tell the eleven-year-old how well her brother Ron had done in the fifth grade. "I don't know whether it's you, or the way they're teaching these days, but your brother never got such poor marks as you bring home," Mother told her.

Emily's poorest marks were in spelling and grammar. She was particularly careless in punctuating sentences and in using plural subjects with singular verbs. Every time her English compositions were returned they looked as if the teacher had cut his finger while marking it. There were large splotches around all the misspelled words and misplaced commas and periods. Other children in the class would have to have been blind not to see how poor Emily's papers were.

One day the teacher said loudly, "Emily, I'm not going to mark your paper at all unless you use a dictionary and a grammar book. Before you hand in one more composition to me, I expect you to do that. Do you understand?"

Emily nodded.

That evening she spent almost two hours checking the spelling of every word in her composition. She also carefully reviewed her punctuation rules and checked them against what she had written on her assignment. This time she would have a perfect paper. Next morning, she got to school early to hand her paper in first. It had been so long since Mr. Abner had praised her work. He was usually so critical and harsh. How comforting it would be to see him look pleasantly at her instead of frowning. How good it would feel to have the other kids hear she did something right for a change.

The praise Emily expected for her perfect paper never materialized. Mr. Abner did not even mention that he was pleased to see that she had overcome her spelling and punctuation errors. He did not compliment her for the hard work she had laboriously put into the accomplishment. Instead, he grumbled, loud enough for most of the children to hear, "Emily, look at the handwriting on this paper! It's practically illegible. If you expect me to give you credit for this work, young lady, you're going to have to write every word of it over again."

Again and again, children are denied the satisfaction of succeeding. As soon as they accomplish one thing, they are immediately shoved on to master the next. In school and at home, some boys and girls rarely get to enjoy the pause that refreshes—the "praise pause." "This is a good spelling job. I knew you could do it." "That's a really hard piano piece; you've done very well with it." "I'm glad to say you handle the car very capably, son!"

More often than not, father *expects* the good and fails to mention the praiseworthy behavior. The only time he opens up his mouth is to criticize when the youngster does something wrong. Frequently, Granny chides the six-year-old for making noise when she's trying to sleep. She never thinks to compliment him on the times he plays quietly. Mother usually takes

Bill's helpfulness around the house for granted; just let the boy drop a dish or misplace a telephone number, however, and she doesn't grant him any respect at all. "Clumsy! . . . You'd probably not know where to find your head if it wasn't attached to your neck!"

No child is successful at everything all of the time. It is unfair to expect him to be. Every child has some talents, some skills, and some assets. Whatever his abilities or attributes, he needs their worth acknowledged. By praising a child's achievements, parents motivate him to work on his faults. Children who feel successful and appreciated feel good enough about themselves to risk challenge. Given the courage to try, they achieve more.

Some boys and girls who seem as if they should be successful are not. Even when they are adequately praised and supported, the recognition does not seem to challenge them to do more. These poorly motivated pupils have lost interest in schoolwork, in their teachers, and in themselves. Some lack the intellectual ability to learn at the same speed, or by the same method, others of their age group do. But they are not incapable of being taught. Many boys and girls have emotional problems, or mental or physical handicaps. But they, too, are neither hopeless nor helpless. There is no reason for them to hear the "No, you're not capable" restraint.

No matter how slow or ill-motivated the learner is, he or she should be encouraged to try. The child should be helped to feel he can succeed. He needs to be carefully encouraged to see himself, not as a problem child, but rather as a child with a problem. Providing the child with a variety of assignments that he can achieve, and matching these to his particular interest and concept level, help him to realize he can succeed. When school and home expectations are designed to meet a youngster's capabilities and interests, he gets a head start in living up to his potential. The following individualized teaching strategies are aimed at the needs of the slow learner or low-motivated child.

1. Teach him or her only a few basic elements of the subject matter at one time.

2. Use constant repetition to emphasize and reinforce specific skills or information.

3. Provide short, clear-cut, complete directions for every task assigned to the child. Don't assume he understands what is expected of him automatically. He might not. Make certain of what he does know by asking him about the task *before* he begins the work.

4. Avoid confusing or frightening the slow learner (or poorly motivated child) with too much too soon. Both the amount of work and the length of time it ought to take him to master it should not burden his short attention span.

5. Don't give long or involved orders, such as "Shovel the front driveway. When you finish, do the steps, clean the windshields on both cars, and put away the sleds. Then bring some wood in for the fire." Remember that reluctant learners comprehend slowly and forget quickly.

6. Supervise closely the self-directed activities of the child. This does not mean being on his back all the time, or reminding him every minute of what he has done or may do wrong. Rather, plan to give the youngster regular guidance and encouragement along the way. He or she will need a lot of it. Compliment his good efforts. If he misunderstands what is expected or how he is to do it, clarify the problem immediately.

7. Organize his periods of study carefully allowing short periods of no more than twelve to fifteen minutes for each task. Before each, help him see how his previous knowledge helps him with the new material.

8. Make clear to the child the purpose and value of what he is learning. "Being able to read better will help you understand the directions for putting a toy together, making a recipe, or using mechanical information in the car manual."

9. Emphasize the importance of social skills and correct habit formation as well as academic performance. Insufficiently motivated boys and girls seem to be generally deficient in the social sensitivity required of their age.

10. Give the child a say in selecting tasks or choosing learning of interest to him. Avoid burdening him with totally adult dominated or designed tasks. Parent-child planning helps children develop the self-confidence they need to plan their own work. Boys and girls are able to learn by doing within a support system they can trust.

One of the best support systems that can be provided for a child is built on the premise that he or she is capable. Parents should believe enough in a child to make him believe in himself. Those who do are much more likely to have successful children. While there is no fail-safe method for motivating boys and girls to become their best, the most successful method known incorporates the following principles.

1. Boys and girls of all ages need to be given challenges and responsibilities in order to experience success. Even if children merely give a task a good try, they learn more than if they make no attempt at all.

2. Success breeds success. The child who is praised for his effort and his achievement develops the courage to keep trying, and succeed in other things.

3. The attitude adults have about a child's capability is reflected in their words, attitude, body language, and actions. When a youngster senses that his parents have no respect for him, or lack confidence in his ability, he thinks he is incapable and acts accordingly.

4. Honest praise helps most children measure up to their potential. When praise is not enough (especially with slow learners and poorly motivated pupils), a variety of special teaching techniques and experiences are required.

Food, clothing, and shelter are physical necessities of life. Love is equally vital for nourishing and protecting the psychological self. Neither man nor child can live by bread alone. Children, in particular, need large amounts of tender loving care. The essence of a child's self-identity is rooted in the quality and quantity of affection, attention, and affirmation he receives. The parent who says "No, I don't love you" utters words of the most frightening magnitude. The child becomes anxious, frustrated, angry, and guilt-ridden. Will Mommy leave him? Will Daddy find some other little girl to love? Would Mom really put an "off limits" on the refrigerator, or refuse to do the laundry, chauffeuring, or message taking? Would Father say, "Get out of the house and see how smart you are on your own," the teenager wonders.

From pre-schooler through adolescence, few children are able to cope with the possibility of having their complete parental support system pulled from under them. The younger the child, the more his parents are all things to him. Mothers and fathers are companions, providers, teachers, protectors. To lose the love of a parent is to be left with nothing at all.

The intensity with which children need parental love is often not understood by adults. If it were, mothers and fathers would never verbalize the withdrawal of love as a threat or punishment, no matter what a child did or said.

* * *

"Dummy! You stupid Mommy. I . . . I hate you, you mean ugly witch lady," five-year-old Eunice shouted vehemently.

"Stop that! One more nasty word out of you and I'm going to wash your mouth out with soap!" Mrs. Rogers replied angrily.

"I don't care!" The little girl sobbed. "You are bad, nasty, dumb, and I . . . don't love you! . . . I hate you . . . because you won't let me go to the circus with Alfred."

"You're a naughty, naughty girl to talk like that to your mommy," Mother's voice rose defensively. "And I don't love you either!"

Eunice's eyes opened wide and terrified. Her mother's words startled her. "Yes you do so love me Mommy!" she insisted.

"No, I don't love you," Mrs. Rogers retorted, emphatically. "You're a bad little girl!"

When love or the withdrawal of love is used as a weapon against children, the war is a war of annihilation. Boys and girls can survive for long periods of time with a minimum amount of food. They can survive even longer with only the bare rudiments of clothing and shelter. Without love, or the assurance of love, children cannot long endure. They exist—they breath, eat, excrete, walk, and talk. They get up in the morning, go to school, and come home again. But they are only going through the motions. Their hearts are not in it; their spirit is gone. The excitement, energy, and enjoyment of living has been sapped from them. Loss of parental affection and affirmation results in loss of self—self-esteem, self-sufficiency, and self-image.

In anger, ignorance, or self-defense, some men and women tell a child they do not love him. Their words and actions impose a cruel and unnatural punishment. The devastating effect of the withdrawal of love from a child is evidenced in the reactions seen in physically abused boys and girls. Children beaten or burned by their parents suffer as much from the emotional implications of the abuse as from the physical. The impact of mother or father not loving them is as painful as the child's black eye or broken bone.

Like Mrs. Rogers, many parents harm children emotionally. They stoop to the child's level to fight. Parents fail to realize how cheap words are to children. Without bothering to have their ears hear what their mouths say, boys and girls spew out hostile, hurtful words. It is their immaturity speaking. Young people do not always activate their brains before they begin to rotate their tongues. Often they are not solely responsible for what they say. Because their choice of words is generated by agitation and anger, what children say at these times should not be taken literally. This doesn't mean that boys and girls should not be held accountable for the way they talk! They should! But parents should also consider the limitations of the child's language before taking offense.

When a three-, eight-, or twelve-year-old shouts, "I hate you!" "Dummy!", or "Jerk!", the remark should be given importance only in relation to the size and maturity of the child uttering it. The smaller the child, the less meaning should be attached to his exact words. Whatever a child's age, he should be seen and heard and listened to carefully. Parents must make it a habit to pay close attention to complaints. What they should not do is take seriously hasty words or insults voiced by the chronologically or emotionally immature.

No matter how men and women react to the taunting or testing of an angry child, they should avoid acting in self-defense. To open fire on a youngster, using the same ammunition he does, does not constitute a fair fight. Mothers and fathers should be physically and emotionally big enough to endure a few barbs. They need to learn to be big enough to handle them intellectually. When the same sharp cutting remarks children use against adults are turned against boys and girls, they become lethal. No matter what their age, or how big a front they put up, children cannot take the same hostility they can give out. Their self-image is not yet secure enough to protect them. Unfortunately, many mothers and fathers don't understand this. They are so deeply hurt by the hostility of their own flesh and blood, they can think of nothing else except to retaliate. This strategy is a backward step in parent-child togetherness.

Six-year-old Doug was petrified of the dark. His terror made the punishment his father used with him even more cruel. When Douglas misbehaved, his dad frequently locked him in the hall closet for five or ten minutes, "to scare out the boy's willfulness," as he put it. There was little chance of physical harm coming to the boy. The closet was large and had sufficient space at the door jamb through which fresh air flowed. The real danger was to Doug's emotional health.

One day, quite accidentally, the boy broke one of his father's favorite blown-glass ornaments. The six-inch replica of an attacking tiger had been perched on the older man's desk. Without asking permission, the son had rummaged through the desk drawer, searching for a rubber band to keep his baseball cards together. The tiger had fallen to the floor and smashed. Dr. Pregman insisted that his son had broken the piece deliberately as a way of getting even with his father for the last punishment. "You knew that was my favorite piece in the collection, didn't you . . . you little . . ."

"No, Dad, No! It was an accident—honest!" Dougie sobbed.

"Accident my foot!" the incensed father roared.

"Well so is this an accident," he shouted, as he took the boy's favorite plastic saxophone and broke it across his knee."

"You broke my saxophone!" the shocked boy screamed, rushing forward to try to piece it together. "You broke it—you dirty stinking rotten rat," he raged at his father.

With one swoop of his large hand, Dr. Pregman grabbed the kicking, screaming boy and put him in the closet. "Now you just stay there where you belong; I don't even want to look at you," Father growled.

In anger and ignorance, some human beings act like animals when they are incensed. They attack. They do not claw or bite, but their actions are destructive, and their words are biting. "I DON'T EVEN WANT TO LOOK AT YOU" . . . "I COULD KILL YOU!" . . . "I WISH YOU HAD NEVER BEEN BORN." . . . "NO, I DON'T LOVE YOU."

"No, I don't love you," was the terrifying thought communicated to an already terrified boy pushed into the dark closet. But if Dr. Pregman were asked at a later date whether or not he loved his son, he surely would have looked quizzically at the inquirer. "Of course, I do: what an odd question to ask! What father doesn't love his own child?"

Many fathers and mothers do not love their own children. Many more act as if they don't. They convey to the child that he is dumb, dishonest, unloved, and unwanted. Whether or not parents mean what they say matters little. The meaning communicated to the child is what counts. Interpreting it word for word, "No, I don't love you!" is difficult to translate any other way than as a denial of affection. What "No, I don't love you" clearly conveys to a boy or girl is absence of affirmation. It is not the kind of absence likely to make a child's heart grow fonder.

* * *

"Well, Miss Smart Ass, how do you feel now? You didn't have a solo part in the school chorus, but you sure managed to have everybody's eyes on you."

Eva lowered her gaze and stared at the kitchen floor.

"You look at me when I talk to you," her mother shouted angrily, pulling the girl's head up by the chin. "I asked you before you left tonight, 'Is that what all the other boys and girls who are singing in the Christmas Choir are wearing on stage . . . blue jeans and blouses?' You said, 'Yes.' I said, 'Eva, why not call Sally . . . just to make sure what she's wearing,' but, NO, that you couldn't bother to do! You were too busy stuffing your face with cupcakes . . . Sooooo . . . what's the result? Your father and I, interested parents that we are, take the trouble to go to the Christmas program and there we are, embarrassed to death . . . What do we see sticking out like a sore thumb on that stage . . . our daughter in blue jeans and a see-through blouse, yet, among thirty decently dressed girls and boys."

"But, Mom . . . I swear . . . I didn't know! Mr. Smith, the chorus master, just said to be sure to come clean and neat. These blue jeans are practically new. I only wore them one time before," the twelve-year-old tried to explain.

"You make me sick," her mother replied angrily. "There your father and I are, among all our neighbors, looking like we can't afford to buy you a skirt . . . or like we're too ignorant to know how to tell you to dress for a holiday program. . . ."

"I'm sorry, Mom, but . . ."

"Who cares about SORRY! Get out of here. Go to your room and stay there, before I. . . ," Mrs. Linn said through clenched teeth.

* * *

Anger and insensitivity never solve a problem between parent and child. They enlarge it. Harsh words and hurt feelings are contagious. The more unlovable the child's action, the more unlovingly her parent responds. The more ill-tempered the parent is, the more hostile the boy or girl becomes. The vicious cycle is self-perpetuating. Only a big person can stop it.

Eva's mother was a lightweight. She was totally inept at pulling her punches. She knew only one method of fighting her daughter—fight to kill. The embarrassment the twelve-year-old's carelessness had caused mother had to be punished in kind. In her own eyes, Mrs. Linn saw that her image among her neighbors had been diminished. Eva had to be belittled and demeaned, too. "Getting even" with children is unacceptable, and it does not show them they are loved. The damage done to boys and girls by cruel, caustic words is sizeable. Words, even more than whippings, cut deep. Insensitive and uncaring barbs undercut the possibility of a wholesome parent-child relationship. Love, respect, and trust between the generations are potent cures for almost anything that ails grown-ups and those growing up. When these daily minimum requirements for well-being are absent, the void is filled with unhealthy suspicions and frustrations.

"I don't care what you say!" Florence screamed. "You do so love him better than me. I'm just nothing to you . . . but a fat little girl with glasses . . . and with dumb pimples, too . . . but *won*derful Josh . . . he's the big star. He's the basketball captain, the honor student, MR. EVERYTHING," she sobbed.

Father shrugged his shoulders in an irritated fashion. The truth hurt. "Now stop that, Florence; stop feeling sorry for yourself just because I caught you in a lie," he cagily avoided the subject. "Your brother

230

didn't leave the car windows open in the rain, YOU
did! . . . and the whole damn back seat looks like
Noah's flood hit it."

"You didn't see ME do it. Josh was sitting in the
back seat, too. Maybe, he left the window open. You
just pick on me because he's your FAVORITE."

Playing favorites is a pastime of many parents. Most of them
don't even know they're participating in a dangerous game.
When there are two or more children in a family, it is rarely
possible to give each one his fair share, all the time. Sometimes
the youngest has to settle for hand-me-down clothes or the toys
of an older sibling. He never receives the rightful portion of new
things that are "all his own." Frequently, one particular child is
saddled with a disproportionate number of responsibilities or
restraints because he's the oldest, or because he should know
better. Often, parental affection is not shared and shared alike.
Sometimes the more demanding, or the more talented, child
commands the lion's share of attention. While his siblings roar
for more, he monopolizes Mom's and Dad's time and energy.
Occasionally, a parent or grandparent will dote on the baby in
the family (even long after he or she is a baby). Sometimes it is
the child wth a physical or learning impairment who is coddled.
Dad may favor his athletically adept son, or the youngster who
is unmistakably a "chip off the old block." Either parent may
gravitate toward the prettiest child, or the one who is most obedient. Without realizing it, mother and father may reject a child
because he or she reminds them of an uncle they didn't like, or
resembles a resented brother or sister of their own. Try, diligent-
ly as they may, many parents do not love all their children equally, or in the same way. They have favorites, and they play favorites, consciously or unconsciously. Sometimes favoritism is
shown when siblings fight or call each other names. Mom invariably steps in and blames one or the other. She metes out verbal
abuse even before she knows what the squabble is about, or who
started it: "Damn you, you little sneak, stop grabbing every-

231

thing away from him. You always have to bother him when all he wants is to play quietly and be left alone." Dad sometimes sets higher standards of behavior for one child than for another. "I do not care how much your Grandfather asks you to do for him, YOU DO IT . . . and without opening your mouth." More often than parents realize, youngsters in the family are treated selectively and inconsistently.

Although most adults refuse to admit that they favor one child over another, they generally do. They do not realize that it is not abnormal or shameful to feel that way. Human beings have preferences, even as far as their own flesh and blood is concerned. Parents who accept, rather than deny, this reality are able to examine their attitudes and actions more intelligently. By seeing what they are doing, mothers and fathers are in a better position to do better. They may not be able to love each child in exactly the same way, but they can learn to love all the children in the family more wisely.

"This is the third time I've had to come to school this semester to talk about why Walt isn't doing well!" Mr. Bernard fumed. "I don't know why in the devil you teachers can't handle these school things yourselves. I don't ask you to control him when he's AT HOME."

Jacquiline Brown, guidance counselor for the seventh grade, held her tongue. She knew it would be useless to argue with the agitated man and woman seated before her.

"I imagine that Walter's teachers think that if we all work together, we could help him more," Mrs. Brown said quietly.

"We can't do anything for him; he's lazy. He'll just have to get up off his fat rear end and do something for himself," the mother replied, looking over at the thin, slouching body of her son.

Thirteen-year-old Walter sat sullen and resentful.

"Look at him over there, will ya!" Mr. Bernard said with contempt. "Does the kid even care that I've had to take another half-day off from work to come up here and see he's not suspended again?"

"I didn't ask ya to come," the boy shot back.

"And you didn't ask to be born, either," Mother retorted sarcastically. "I know that story already. . . . We should all feel sorry for you kids because, after all, you didn't ask to be put on this ugly, cruel, boring earth. Well, I'm not feeling one bit sorry for you. The only one I'm sorry for is myself. I'm sorry we ever decided to adopt you. . . . You've been nothing but trouble since you first came to live with us ten years ago."

"Ya had your chance to think about THAT a long time ago," Father interrupted.

"You know, Mrs. Brown," Walter's mother continued angrily, addressing herself to the counselor. "My husband here warned me, and he never lets me forget it. I wish I had listened. . . . He said, 'Look, Matilda, we have three nice girls of our own; we can be a happy family without a son . . . but . . . I wanted a little boy and . . . look at him NOW. Lord, how I wish I had listened to you, Harley," the woman sighed, as she turned toward her husband.

More and more parents would do well to listen to each other. They ought to listen to themselves, too. Men and women should pay careful attention to what they are saying to children. Do boys and girls get the message that mom and dad understand them, or want to understand them? Do the youngsters feel they are respected and trusted? Do children of every age know in no uncertain terms that they are liked and loved by their parents— even when their behavior is unacceptable? The animosity and disgust conveyed by Walter's parents could in no way be mistaken. It was rejection of both his actions and him. He was trouble:

an ingrate, a burden. They wished they had never gotten him in the first place.

In moments of frustration and anger, many men and women say things they do not mean. But just as a bell cannot be unrung, words, once said, cannot be unsaid. Their sound lingers on in the child's memory. Uncaring, hostile words accumulate one upon the other. While a few thoughtless words can be tolerated by the child, too many become a burden beyond his ability to assimilate.

> Teresa carried the idea around in her head that her parents didn't care about her. Poppa had warned her time and time again, in no uncertain terms, that she would have to shape up or ship out. Momma was always saying, "Now look here, you, you're not gonna skip no more school. And you're not gonna get away with hiding one more of those cigarettes in your room."
>
> "You tell her, Mary," Father chimed in. "And a girl like you from a good family isn't gonna hang around with that wild crowd anymore, either."
>
> "You hear your father, Teresa?" Mother added. "If you'd rather be with them—with those friends of yours—all the time, if you don't think this house is good enough, then find someplace else to live, and see how you like it."

When the sixteen-year-old actually ran away from home, her parents didn't understand what had happened—or why. They had *not really meant* what they said. They had never in their wildest imagination intended to give her the choice to stay home or leave and live someplace else. All that was just talk. It was what mothers and fathers said to kids to scare them a little and make them open their eyes to how good they had it at home. Momma's and Poppa's words were just a threat. But they were uttered so loudly and clearly that Teresa took her parents at their word. She did not understand that they were not able to convey effectively what they actually meant to say. As the communication lines between the adults and their only child became more and more closed, they felt that they couldn't reach her. When Terry ran away, parental disbelief turned to anxiety. Then it turned to anger. "How could she do this to us when we've sacrificed our lives for her?" Momma sobbed. "Just let me get my hands on her!" Poppa threatened.

When a child runs away from home it is important for parents to get their hands on her as soon as possible. The hands should not be used for hitting, but rather for helping. Whatever difficulties arise once a child is brought home from an inappropriate escapade, scolding and shaming should be very limited. What was done is done. The important thing left to do is show her how worried her parents were. Mother and father need to explain to the child that she was missed, that they are glad and grateful to have her back. The anger and intensity of feeling that clogged their lines of communication in the first place should be examined. New lines of trust, respect, and understanding need to be built. Talking *with* Teresa, rather than at her, would help. Greater parental understanding of changing times and the stress this places on children is also important. Parents do not have to see eye-to-eye with their children, but they should try, as much as possible, to look at life through the youngster's eyes. This approach enables mothers and fathers to guide children appropriately. By knowing where children are, physically and emotionally, parents can avoid jumping to conclusions, or not taking action at all, until it's too late. The most indestructibly healthy foundation for the parent-child relationship is contained in the words and actions which assure boys and girls that they are loved. Love may not in reality conquer all things, but it does build a base of strength from which parent and child, together, can enjoy a more wholesome, happy, relationship.

1. All children, regardless of their age, need to feel they are loved. Parental affection and affirmation nour-

ish and protect the child's psychological self in the same way food, clothing, and shelter sustain his physical body.

2. Parents who threaten to withdraw love from the child inflict a cruel and unnatural punishment on him. Even when boys and girls act unlovingly and uncaringly toward their parents, the adults should be mature enough to avoid resorting to "getting even."

3. The misbehavior of the child should always be carefully separated from what he is, in and of himself. Behavior can be totally unacceptable at the same time that the child is accepted and affirmed.

4. Many adults refuse to admit they play favorites between children in the family. The tendency is neither abnormal nor shameful. When it is understood and accommodated, each boy and girl in a family can be loved well and more wisely.

12.

WHEN "NO" IS ENOUGH TO SHOW YOU CARE

In the story of Peter Pan, a little fairy named Tinker Bell loved Peter so much that she was willing to die for him. Evil Captain Hook was determined to kill Peter; he had secretly put poison in the little boy's medicine bottle. Unable to warn her friend, Tinker Bell swallowed the liquid herself, to save Peter.

The love parents have for their children is rarely tested in such a dramatic way. But the affection they feel is just as strong and unselfish. Most mothers and fathers love their sons and daughters very much. Unfortunately, not all of them know the right way to show it. Some adults are unsuccessful because they are prisoners of the past, constrained by their own upbringing. Other parents fail because they are captives of the present. The day-to-day pressures of parenthood are so overwhelming that mothers and fathers often become sullen and silent. Rushed and resentful, they are unable to express their affection for their children fully. Other men and women are victims of fantasy. They mistakenly give youngsters an excess of love and insufficient limits.

Parents who are prisoners of the past were probably not loved wisely or well themselves. Most were regularly threatened, abused, or ignored. Their own parents knew very little about the human growth and development principles upon which a wholesome, happy parent-child relationship is built. Hit therapy was the order of the day! Boys and girls of every age were whipped, walloped, yelled at, and belittled. When a child needed his parents the most, he was likely to be ignored and neglected. Some children became scapegoats for the dissatisfaction and inadequacy their mothers and fathers felt; they were deliberately and callously denied adult attention or affection. When those sons and daughters grew to adulthood, they quite naturally became the kind of mothers and fathers their parents had been. They did unto their own offspring as had been done unto them. Whenever they had to "knock some sense into the kid's head, for his own good," they had no qualms about knocking him around, or giving him a few good slaps across the face to do it. After all, wasn't this the way their parents had to treat them? Physical punishment was the way to show the child you cared enough about him to "straighten him out." Otherwise, why would their own parents, who surely loved them, have used it?

Not by their choice do parents treat their children unfairly and uncaringly. Many do what they do for lack of choice. Improper role models showed them how love for children should be expressed. Nobody taught them any other way to be a mother or a father.

The men and women who are captives of the present frequently mistreat boys and girls, too, but for a different reason. Having children has turned out to be more pain than pleasure. The job of parenting has failed to materialize into the joy of parenthood as it was supposed to. The real and rigorous responsibilities of being with children, caring for them, disciplining them, day by day and week after week have proved to be overwhelming. Adult time, energy, and even solvency are exhausted by the many demands made by boys and girls. The added pressure of a destructured society, with the absence of family support systems, also creates emotional wear and tear. Trying to earn a living, satisfy relatives and friends, and find some time for one's self proves physically and psychologically draining. Mothers and fathers more than other adults have trouble juggling all the competing demands for their attention and effort. Little wonder that the full expression of the love they feel for their children gets lost in the shuffle.

Like the captives of the present and the prisoners of the past, men and women who are the victims of fantasy find no real success or joy as parents. They communicate their love through halo therapy. Children are treated as if they are fragile little angels who can do no wrong. "No" is rarely said; it is considered too dictatorial and constraining. In the give-and-take relationship between parent and child, the adult does all the giving, and the boy or girl all the taking. Mothers and fathers voluntarily put themselves down—as doormats. Naturally, children do what is expected of them. They walk all over the adults.

There are several reasons why grown men and women lower themselves to the level of children. None of the reasons are good ones. Some adults are afraid their youngster will not love them if he is made to follow parental rules. Mothers and fathers are so terrified by the possibility of being rejected that they never stand up to boys or girls. Some childishly cater to the whims and the will of their offspring for another reason: The child is seen as a mystical extension of the parental self. The existence of Debbie and Joey give Mother and Dad a second chance. They are able to relive their own lives through their children. Grown men and women can do many of the things they wanted to do but never had the chance: Through the reflected glory of their son's artistic ability, or their daughter's athletic achievements, they themselves can rise and shine. Similar permissive treatment of children is practiced by parents who wish to generate creativity in their offspring. Mistakenly, they believe that by letting a child do whatever he wants, he is more likely to do something original. To restrain him in any way from doing his own thing might restrict him from reaching his full, individual potential. No matter how different the reasons for permissive handling of children, they share one similarity: They are all wrong. Permissive parents avoid what they see as frustrating to the child; they decline to burden him with responsibility by saying "no." As victims of fantasy, these adults are unable to be successful parents in the real world. They harm both themselves and their children.

Neither halo therapy nor hit therapy is a logical and loving way to raise children. One is too heavily child-centered; the other too top-heavy with adult control. Both fail to provide the kind of structure boys and girls need. They also prevent the adults from feeling good about themselves. One burdens them with being tyrants; the other, with being "taken." Children who are killed with kindness resent their parents. They show this by continuing to take more and more advantage. They challenge Mom and Dad to have the courage and the concern to say "no." When adults do not use this tiny word, the respect and love they want from their children is lost. Consciously or subconsciously, adults know how weak they look in the eyes of their sons and daughters. They lose respect for themselves, too, a loss of respect which generates resentment. Whenever men and women are compelled, for whatever reason, to give in more and more to a child, they feel taken. On the other hand, when boys and girls are handled too punitively, they grow to despise adults for their insensitivity. They resent the unfairness and harshness with which they are treated. Sometimes a child's resentment causes him to repeat the forbidden action over and over again, just to get even. His anger is so intense that it blocks out any remorse for the misbehavior, even the possibility of a lesson being learned. Punitive parents, too, are the victims of anger. They are angry both at their children and at themselves. What upsets them most is their inability to feel good about their relationship with their youngsters. Big as they are, and aggressive as they act, deep down inside, such men and women feel small and inadequate. They are agitated and drained of good humor. Long after the "mad" they feel against the child is expended, they continue to harbor a "mad" feeling toward themselves.

Time and time again, the too-much-too-soon and the too-little-too-late methods of child rearing have failed. Only one method of parent-child relationship has the psychological soundness to satisfy both age groups. The method is BACK TO BALANCE—a balance that takes account of the needs and wants and rights and responsibilities of both parents and children. At heart this balance is neither rigid nor formlessly flexible. Flexibility exists, but it is flexibility within structure. This combination provides enough support to bring adult and child together while providing enough leeway to accommodate the individuality of each. A well-balanced relationship between adults and children is rooted in the use of "no" as a love word. When grown-ups apply the right "no," at the right time, spoken in the right way, they discipline children in the best way possible. They guide boys and girls, FAIRLY, FIRMLY, CONSISTENTLY, AND CARINGLY. The four "no's" on which adults should rely—THE LIFE SAVING "NO," THE CHALLENGE "NO," THE CHARACTER-BUILDING "NO," and THE CONVENIENCE "NO"—have their proper place in the lives of boys and girls of every age. Parents should use them regularly and without guilt. Conversely, the three "No's" which it is imperative to avoid are, "No, I won't listen;" "No, you're not capable," "No I don't love you."

Not only adults, but those growing up should know clearly and confidently that "no" is not an enemy. Thoughtful limit setting by parents does not restrict a youngster's life, it enhances it. Setting children on the right road toward self-discipline and achievement brings them self-respect, strength of character, and joy. They are protected from detouring into the

241

dead ends of instant gratification, ignorance, and ineffectiveness. At every age boys and girls should be helped to understand the four "no's." With patience and self-assurance, men and women should share with young people an understanding of which "no" is being applied in a particular situation and why.

"I'm sorry, honey, you may not make cookies at our house with your friend before I get home from work. The stove has a very unreliable pilot light, and I don't want to take any chance of your lighting a match or getting hurt when there is no adult around to help you." This "no" is a life-saving "no."

"Richard, you know you promised your sister that today you'd teach her how to work your computerized toy and play Scrabble. You can't go over to your friend's, instead, just because the kids are playing Ping-Pong there. Difficult as it sometimes is, when people give their word, they have to keep it. I know, I understand you'd rather be with your friends than with her, but you promised, and she's your sister, besides. That's what loyalty means." This is a character building "no."

"I've talked it over with Mother, and we agree that you can't use the birthday money you got from Grandfather to buy your friend's ten-speed bike. There's nothing wrong with your three-speed. If you're still determined to trade it in for the ten-speed, you'll have to find some other way to get the forty dollars. There are a lot of ways you might earn the money, but I think that's up to you. Give it some thought. No, I'm not going to tell you how." This is a challenge "no."

"Rhonda, I know it's your room, but we're having company, and they'll be all over the house. We may well have to use your room to put the coats and hats in. I've spent a lot of time preparing for this party, and I would prefer it if people didn't think that I keep a sloppy house . . . I want you to clean your room now . . . I said, 'I knew it was your room,' but nevertheless, straighten it up now please." This is a convenience "no."

Giving the child a reason, even if what is said is not exactly what he wanted to hear, gives him the respect to which he is entitled. It tells him that thought and logic have gone into the adult decision. His parents aren't laying down rules in haste. Nor are they just trying to show who is boss. They care about him and his physical and psychological well-being. They care enough to take the time to give him their best—CONSTRUCTIVE, JUST, CARING DISCIPLINE.

No matter how conscientious or skilled parents are, they are not able to forestall every inappropriate behavior exhibited by their child. Nor should they attempt to. Adults know they cannot win all the time; children need victories too. Two criteria apply to winning and losing: whether the child's action or attitude poses a real danger to himself or others, and whether the adult can "live with" the youngster's misbehavior. If restraint is called for in a lifesaving situation, the "no" should be non-negotiable, as it is in the following examples: "No" to hitchhiking; "No" to going off with a stranger; "No" to playing with matches, guns, or sharp objects; "No" to the abuse of mind or body with drugs, alcohol, and sexual promiscuity.

The particular incident, and the stress it places on adults, determines whether it is wise to implement the convenience "no." Different things irritate different people. Some parents are perfectly able to live with noise, sullenness, back talking, or laziness on occasion; others cannot tolerate these conditions at all.

The application of the challenge "no" and the character-building "no" are also governed by the balance between adult

243

needs and children's needs. In bringing balance and trust to the parent-child relationship, the adult is wise to *give in* at the right time. In disciplining children, not only the immediate situation, but its long-term effect should be considered. Boys and girls who are permitted to win their fair share of the less vital decisions are more willing to accept parental leadership in the more important onces. When adults foolishly refuse to let the child win any argument, or will not tolerate behavior that is less than exemplary, they sacrifice long-term success for a short-term victory.

Each day parents are faced with the responsibility of deciding whether to restrict or permit certain behavior in a child. The soundest and easiest way to gain a balanced relationship between "allowing" and "limiting" is through the use of the SEVEN NO'S STRATEGY. This is a strategy based on structure, not on control. Control leads to rigidity, imbalance of authority, and failure. Whether the controlling force is parent or child, a harmful lack of equilibrium exists in the relationship. Structure means flexibility within reasonable limits. Both the limitations and the logic of their use is understood and accepted by both parent and child. The integrity of the adults and of those growing up are upheld by this well-structured support system.

With the answers to the following questions, parents can use their common sense to decide whether they are controlling or structuring their children's lives. Structuring which is fair, firm, consistent, and caring creates balance.

THE SEVEN NO'S STRATEGY

1. Is the child given enough time to be both seen and heard? Is his side of a request or disagreement expressed, or is the youngster shut up and shut out of the decision-making process?

2. Is the "no" in question one of the three that should be avoided? If it is, change it. If any of these "no's" have already been said, seek out the child and admit a mistake was made. Parents should not be afraid to admit they were hasty or wrong. Children respect honesty in adults. This also teaches them to be honest and unafraid of making mistakes. Boys and girls think more of adults who admit their errors than of those who try to cover them up.

3. Is the "no" appropriate to the particular situation in which it is used? A lifesaving "no" would be warranted if a child tried to put his hand through the bars of a lion's cage. It would also be valid, after the fact, if a boy took a six-pack of beer from the refrigerator and drank it when his parents were not home. The same kind of restraint would not be appropriate if the child merely wanted to get a closer look at the lion. Nor would a lifesaving "no" make sense for a child who wanted to have a glass of wine with his parents who were celebrating some special occasion.

4. Is the child told the reason for the "no"? The age of the child, the incident, and the specific "no" used often determine whether or not an explanation is possible. If the reason for the limit cannot be given before the fact, it is helpful to give it afterward. "I didn't have time to tell you why I yelled 'no' and pushed you away from the sink when you tried putting water on the grease fire in the stove. Water puts out most fires, but it spreads fires which are caused by grease."

5. Is the "no" said in a caring way? Is ridicule or sarcasm ever used? Is the adult tone of voice, body language, volume of voice, firm but friendly—or authoritarian and unfriendly?

6. Is the child given a chance to respond to the deci-

sion made? Even when his comments would have no effect at all on what the adult has determined, it is supportive to let the child have the last word sometimes. Lines of communication are kept open in this way.

7. In reanalyzing the situation, was a "no" answer necessary? How many "yes's" has the child been given that day or that week? In striving to reach a balance, was the particular situation important enough to choose a "no," or would "yes" have been a wiser choice?

Use of the SEVEN NO'S STRATEGY on a regular basis helps parents learn from their mistakes. The knowledge that can be gained from the procedure contributes to greater satisfaction and security for everyone. Careful explanation of which "no" is which helps the child develop a sense of organization and logic. By learning the kinds of limits his parents see fit to impose upon him, he learns what to reject and avoid by himself. He understands more fully why it is right or wrong to behave in a certain way. This understanding is the foundation of his growth in self-discipline. Self-control in children develops best when they are given a solid model or structure to follow. Boys and girls learn how to control themselves through the practice given them by parents. When the preadolescent begins to move away from dependence on adults to dependence on self and peers, he carries with him the indelible mark of the family attitudes and values he has come to respect and trust. Children of all ages have nowhere to grow if nothing is expected of them.

Self-discipline, self-sufficiency, and social responsibility are nurtured in boys and girls whose parents LOVE THEM, LISTEN TO THEM, LIMIT THEM and LET THEM GO. Children should be given attention and affection, structure, and freedom. From birth through young adulthood, young people search for a security blanket to keep them safe and warm. Until they grow big enough and wise enough to confidently venture out into the world on their own, boys and girls need the psychological comfort provided by caring, sharing, self-assured adults. Children need to feel their parents' own strength of purpose in guiding them. Boys and girls believe in adults who believe in themselves.

Men and women who develop the will and the way to discipline children feel better about themselves. They have no fear in dealing with boys and girls, no matter how trying or serious the confrontation may be. Secure parents are secure enough to communicate "Yes, I will listen to you." Nor do they hesitate to insist to the child of any age, "And now, you, Johnny, in turn will hear me out, with the same mutuality of respect and trust I gave to you. We will both give-and-take in our relationship. We will try to understand each other better and to build a togetherness which will support and satisfy us."

The support and satisfaction required by children mandates that mother and father convey the message, in their own words: "Yes, I will listen, and yes I love you. I don't always like your behavior or your attitude; I get angry just like you do, and tired and overwhelmed. Sometimes I say things I wish I hadn't, but let me say now that what is true, no matter how irritated or frustrated you get me, is that *I love you.* The feeling of love is basic and irreversible. When I do not approve of your behavior, when I cannot allow you to ruin your life or grow up undisciplined, you will have to conform to set rules. You must change your behavior sometimes, promptly and maturely. It will be hard for you to believe that because I love you, I am limiting you. It will take your best effort to change and learn self-control, but I believe in you and will help as much as I can."

Helping children adhere to limits and learn self-control is the most precious gift parents can give them. It is the gift of life—a balanced, productive life rather than a restless, rootless one. Fairness, firmness, and consistency are the food, water, and air of a child's social, emotional, and intellectual health. Lacking any one, boys and girls are improperly nour-

247

ished. Their full growth is stunted. The child who is aided by an adult to understand and accept behavioral restraints is able to use his energy more effectively. He does not waste time fighting parents every inch of the way. The youngster desists from trying to test or challenge even the most sensible limits they set. Boys and girls raised within the framework of NO AS A LOVE WORD, with the four "no's" that should be said and the three that should not, are well-disciplined. They are less likely to pursue inappropriate or dangerous whims and wants, even when they are no longer under the watchful eye of their mothers and fathers. Given the proper amount of flexibility within structure, they have room both to assert themselves and grow, while complying with overall directions set for them. Security and satisfaction result from this balance. The youngster develops the ability to handle the decisions which are his to make. The competence and confidence gained enable him to follow the leadership of adult direction when parental decisions are appropriate. The child learns to respect the basic fact that there is a balance between his rights and those of his parents. Another balance exists between the privileges he is given and his responsibility to use them intelligently. Freedom is not the right to do whatever he wants, but the privilege to do what is right and fair to both himself and others. The right way for a child to become an intelligent and independent adult is to be reared in a family which disciplines him properly. Although every child is different, and every parent, too, the proper disciplinary structure is the same. Not only should children be guided fairly, firmly, consistently, and caringly, but they should be punished, when that is necessary, in the same way.

BE FIRM

Children need and want guidance. They want to know their exact boundaries and limitations. Having settled on the kind of behavior expected, do not chicken out. If re-examination of the behavioral standard set subsequently indicates that you were too hard-boiled, soften your stance. When the necessity arises, punish firmly, even if it hurts you more than the child.

BE CONSISTENT

Having set the rules for the desired forms of behavior, exercise them regularly. Inconsistency is as dangerous as the lack of structure. The child who is allowed to do something one time and forbidden to do it the next becomes totally disoriented. He also can become immobilized and afraid to do anything for fear that he might do the wrong thing.

BE CARING

Talk to the child. Never shut him out or shut him up until he has had his say. Always give him a chance to explain why he acted in a particular manner. Try to understand his logic and reasons in terms of his age and experiences. Adult punishment frequently penalizes children for doing what is normal for their level of development. When speaking, use a tone of voice and a degree of patience which show care.

Men and women who care enough about themselves and their children are not afraid to discipline them. Structuring the lives of children is both a parental right and responsibility. From the preschool years through adolescence boys and girls need and want directions. Discipline teaches them to become self-controlled and self-respecting. The lesson that "no" is a love word is both simple and profound. It communicates to children this message:

You are important. Your ideas count. Your needs count. As your parent, I may not always understand you, nor you me, but I am always here to listen, to love you, to support you, to help you structure your life. Here . . . let me show you.